"Like a well-crafted novel, I was drawn in by the story, which moves with pace and interesting characters, but Pletcher gives us so much more. The sustained impact of *Henry's Glory* is the way in which marketplace leaders are encouraged and motivated to see their work as their worship to God. Don't treat this as another novel, it's a life-shaping experience."

—CRAIG SIDER
President, The New York City Leadership Center

"To know and serve Jesus is essential to the Christian life. I love how Dr. Pletcher stirs up our desire to serve Christ in the workplace. This book will challenge you to do exactly that—wherever you work and whatever you do each day."

—DOUG FUNK
Vice President, D. H. Funk and Sons LLC

"Despite the Apostle Paul's teaching that everyone in the body of Christ is needed, many Christians see themselves as inferior contributors to the life of the body. . . . *Henry's Glory* . . . not only debunks this insidious belief, but also provides a proven way for church leaders to help all Christians know and live out their God-given value within the body of Christ."

—PAUL D. BORDEN
Author of *Make or Break Your Church in 365 Days*

"*Henry's Glory* adds a helpful, believable narrative to the growing body of literature on the relationship of faith and work. John is a gifted writer who knows how to communicate important theological concepts through interesting and accessible narrative. I hope students of business and theology, as well as workplace leaders everywhere, will seriously consider reading and implementing the captivating vision John presents!"

—DON J. PAYNE
Associate Professor of Theology
and Christian Formation, Denver Seminary

"I wholeheartedly recommend this Christ-honoring, creative resource. *Henry's Glory* will prove thought-provoking and deeply motivating for pastors, small groups, and students everywhere. Enjoy the story and join God in your workplace! You will experience a serious jump-start to everyday, missional living."

—ALAN ROBINSON
National Director of the Brethren in Christ Church in the U.S.

"Pletcher has offered a marvelous example of my favorite kind of writing, a compelling story that communicates deeper truths. . . . I would encourage small groups to read and study this book together, if for no other reason than that most churches aren't talking about this, and should be."

—ANTHONY L. BLAIR
President, Evangelical Seminary, Pennsylvania

"John challenges the conventional thinking that in order for our daily work to have significance, it must flow from or through an organized religious entity. Through the story of a young man's quest for meaning and purposeful living, he helps us see the importance of our individual role in God's big story. Our daily work is a key component for impacting others in some of the most meaningful ways."

—TRACY SEIGER
Realtor, Prudential Homesale Services

"Regardless of one's profession, the story inspires us to not compartmentalize between the sacred and secular, but instead to participate in 'God's original intention for creation to involve healthy, creative work.'"

—DALE R. YODER
AIA, President, Cornerstone Design Architects

"Soak up this story! *Henry's Glory* offers a fresh perspective on the purpose and value of work, challenging assumptions about what is sacred and what is secular. If you've ever wondered if there is meaning and lasting value in what you do every day, I highly recommend it!"

—JOHN COX
Executive Vice President, Turkey Hill Dairy

Henry's Glory

Henry's Glory

*A Story for Discovering Lasting Significance
in Your Daily Work*

JOHN ELTON PLETCHER

RESOURCE *Publications* · Eugene, Oregon

HENRY'S GLORY
A Story for Discovering Lasting Significance in Your Daily Work

Resource Publications
An Imprint of Wipf and Stock Publishers
199 W. 8th Ave., Suite 3
Eugene, OR 97401

www.wipfandstock.com

ISBN 13: 978-1-62564-293-6

Manufactured in the U.S.A.

To my mother, Holly
& my father, Kenny

They have inspired me across the years with a passion for exploration and communication of God's precious truths. Dad was very enthusiastic when I first shared with him the focus of this project. He graduated to glory before it was completed. I praise God for Mom and Dad's legacy—their own deep love for God, his loving story, and his mission to reach more people for his kingdom.

Contents

Introduction

Your Faith at Work

The story in your hands was written for grease-covered car guys, running-fast real estate gals, plumbers, pastors, farmers, entrepreneurs, teachers, busy soccer moms, CEOs, and everybody else who is working so hard day after day.

More and more people are longing to know, *How does my everyday job, where I spend so many crazy hours of my life, connect to God's larger story and his purposes in the world?*

Bigger thinkers—people like you, willing to read books like this one—are asking bigger questions about their life calling. You are probably wondering if your *real work* every day can have significant meaning for advancing Christ's kingdom, his great mission. I imagine that down in your soul, you've been hoping that what you do in your workplace could count for something more in the grand scheme. And you're still wondering . . .

Your journey through these pages will lead you on an adventure of discovery, chasing after answers to these very questions! I wrote this story for you, with the deep-in-my-heart hunch that Christ wants each of us to *be the church, on his mission* every day.

You can maximize this resource by letting yourself get fully wrapped up in the twists and turns. By all means, *enjoy* the story—but pause enough at the end of each chapter to thoughtfully process discussion questions as well as recommended attitude shifts and action points. Resist your urge to rush ahead. Read each suggested Scripture passage and think about its meaning. Personalize your answers to the questions, aiming for genuine, real-life application. Challenge yourself to intentionally create follow-up action steps in response to what you have read. In addition, you will experience more from this story by discussing it with your small group, a book club, or a circle of friends at your local coffee shop. Indulge in laughing, thinking, and learning together.

It is my heartfelt prayer that you deeply engage with this story and allow it to impact your own story in your workplace—all for Christ's glory!

John Elton Pletcher
Lancaster, Pennsylvania
Fall 2013

CHAPTER ONE

A Disturbing Piece of Poetry

Fireflies sparkled across the steamy-hot, nighttime sky. Zach had retreated to the seat in the old pickup truck some twenty minutes ago, escaping the noisy congestion of his grandparents' house. His mind and emotions were spinning. Air conditioning was supposed to be cooling Grandma's house, but the air inside was thick with worrisome tears and frayed nerves. For these moments, Zach found some ironic sanctuary on the cracked vinyl bench of the '77 Ford F-100. He rolled down the windows.

"At least these still work," Zach sarcastically mused as he cranked on the archaic window knobs. "Not like anything else on this heap of junk does. Why in the world did he *insist* on giving me this jalopy?"

Grandma's place was crawling with his cousins, their kids, Zach's mom and dad, plus a gaggle of family members he had not seen in over a decade. Doctors had speculated that Grandpa had two to three days, maybe five if he was lucky. It was now day seven. It seemed that Grandpa had rallied back again. Inside the house, various family members were engaged in heated dialogue. *Stay around to wait and see, or pack up and head back home? After all, who knows how long he might hold on? He's always been just a little too stubborn.*

Zach hated such internal wrangling, both for his family members and for his own soul. He had already taken five days off work. Running both hands through his brownish blonde, curly-thick hair,

Zach exhaled and pounded the steering wheel. He shouted into the air, "I just want this to be over and my life back to normal!"

Larry, founder and lead architect at the firm, had been more than accommodating when Zach had asked for time to go say goodbye to his dying grandfather. Now, the young architect's thoughts tormented him. *I have SO much to tackle back in the office. Should I go? Should I stay a few more days?* In reality, his internal issues ran much deeper than yet-to-conquer work deadlines. In the face of his grandfather's grave illness, Zach was wrestling with his own questions about his own eternal significance.

He was in year eight, having come to Brinkley Design-Build in Valley Forge, Pennsylvania, two years after completing college. Garnering the respect of Larry Brinkley and five other senior designers had been no small feat. But across the years, Zach had brought innovative style, bold lines, and something of an ancient-future approach to his commercial projects. As the youngest architect on the team, he was admired for his playful panache and creative use of bold color. Most of all, it was his amazing drive to tackle a host of new projects each year, yielding robust revenues, that earned him the respect of his aging colleagues.

In spite of how late it was and the long week, Maggie's eyes still sparkled. Zach could not deny that her vivacious smile and beautiful blond hair were a welcome addition to the gloomy pickup cab.

Only recently had the firm's work begun to sputter with the doggish economy. Zach's team members, including boss Larry, had started showing signs of desperation during the past nine months. At times, Zach sensed they were cutting corners, promising big, underbidding, but then delivering less than they had promised clients. And he knew for certain their entire work environment was markedly different, much more stressful and relationally antagonistic.

Now, with his grandfather fading, plus this groundswell of thoughts and feelings from the previous months, he was starting to wonder how much of this, if any of this, really mattered anyway. *Should I remain in this field? I LOVE design work, but is it really what I'm supposed to be doing with my life?* And tonight, his heart was circling inside like twister winds in a summer storm.

Thump, thump. The pound on the passenger's side door jolted Zach from his subterranean thinking. Maggie grinned through the glass. "Scared you, didn't I? Let me in." He stretched across the seat and lifted the chipped off, well-worn lock. She jumped in.

"What are you doing out here?" she asked. "Your mom sent me to find you. You OK?"

In spite of how late it was and the long week, Maggie's eyes still sparkled. Zach could not deny that her vivacious smile and beautiful blond hair were a welcome addition to the gloomy pickup cab.

"Yea, just trying to think," Zach replied. "You know, it's a lot to process."

Maggie had volunteered to join Zach on the eight-hour trek from Pennsylvania to Ohio last week. They'd been friends since middle school, though no one could precisely define their relationship. Across high school and college, they had both seriously dated other people off and on. Through the roller coaster of other relationships, they kept in touch with each other and made sure to keep their good friendship rolling.

Her closest friends just called her Mags for short.

When oft-teased about being with Zach, she always informed her girlfriends that she and Zach were just "too good a friends to be a dating couple." And then she would add, "He's always there for me, like a great big brother. That's it. Why mess that up?"

When oft-teased about being with Zach, she always informed her girlfriends that she and Zach were just "too good a friends to be a dating couple." And then she would add, "He's always there for me, like a great big brother. That's it. Why mess that up?"

And friends and family always smiled, and they thought there just had to be something more to it. Maybe.

Maggie's dad was Larry Brinkley. Zach's hire at Brinkley Design after college, followed by his virtual rock-star status in the company, had thrust he and Maggie into constant interaction once again. Nine years back, Maggie had started a mobile veterinary clinic, a business that now included five fully-equipped Sprinter vans and four additional vets. Her great love had been animals, creatures in every incarnation, ever since she was tiny. Out of college, Dad had backed her with both bright business insights and big bucks. In return, during weekends and other spare time, Mags took project pictures and helped drive marketing initiatives for the design firm.

She had loved photography since the first time she looked through a camera as a seven-year old, and she was good at seeing and snapping what others didn't see. Consequently, everything Zach first saw in his mind and designed for clients was eventually captured through Mags' lens. Zach's designs had won awards. Mags' pics had won them new customers up and down the east coast, and even some unique work in Spain as well as South America.

"So, what are you thinking?" Maggie asked. "Can I help, or do you want to be alone? I can go tell your mom you're fine." She reached for the dusty door handle.

"No, *stay*! *Stay* right here!" Zach commanded.

"Wow, your canine command is convincing. Should I also sit and shake?" Mags quipped back with quirky vet humor.

"I'm sorry. Didn't mean to sound bossy." Zach realized how short he'd sounded. "Seriously sorry. I'm just feeling the pressure. I really don't want to lose him. I said my goodbyes this morning. And I know he's headed to a better place. He's ready to go. But how long is he going to hold on? And everybody inside that house is *so* tense about everything."

"I know," Mags reassured. "Really wish I could change things for you. Your family is amazing, and they really care. I've always admired that. All that care is showing up right now as worry and anxiety. I just wish I could do something more to help."

Zach shot back, "You *have*, Mags. Look, you're sitting here next to me and going through this with me. You're doing a lot. 'Truth is, I'm mixed up right now about a bunch of stuff. Yes, I'm so sad about Grandpa's condition, but it's more than that."

"OK, so *what*? You can tell me. I know things aren't ideal for you at work right now. We talked about those pieces as we drove the whole state of Pennsylvania the other night. So what is it? What else?"

"It's my uncle. He's bugging me again." Zach exhaled. "As the bunch of us walked out of Grandpa's hospital room this morning, Uncle Clyde said it again. 'Drives me crazy. He first said it to me back when I was eleven or maybe twelve years old. He said it to me the night I got Honors Society in tenth grade, and then again at both high school and college graduations." Zach grimaced and ran his fingers through his hair.

Uncle Clyde was known to everyone outside the family as *Brother Clyde*. He was a larger-than-life kind of person, over-the-top, opinionated, and pretentious, especially with family and close friends. Recognized as a preacher man, Clyde was known by many folks across the county for his zealous, fiery oratory in the pulpit. He carried a large, stocky physique, always cloaked in suit and tie, with silvery, slicked back hair. Gospel Holiness Chapel was tucked up in the woods, just south of Route 40. Clyde had pastored there since he was seventeen years old.

Brother Virgil, the previous pastor, had preached at Gospel Holiness for over thirty-five years. In its prime, the Chapel drew over three hundred people, although mostly on revival meeting weeks. As a teenager, Clyde had shown some promising potential when he preached in a couple youth services on Sunday nights. With Pastor Virgil's sudden heart attack, the church's deacons sensed Clyde's call and offered him the position within a week of their beloved preacher's going to heaven. That next Sunday morning, they laid their hands on Clyde, anointed and ordained him. That was thirty-two years ago. In the past decade, the church had declined and now sputtered along with just under one hundred people. In spite of such decline, Brother Clyde was still somewhat famous and widely known across three adjoining counties.

"What?" Mags probed. "What did he say? You've never told me about this."

Zach responded. "Uncle Clyde says, with great bravado, 'Only one life, 'twill soon be past. Only what's done for Christ will last.' One of those times I asked him if he made that up, and he said it came from an old missionary. But for the life of me, I can't remember who originally said it. And I'm not sure that he remembers."

Mags and Zach both chuckled.

"So why does that bother you so much?" she asked.

"Well, because I know what he is more than implying."

"And what's he implying?" Maggie probed. "Divine it for me, oh revealer of deep mysteries."

"Very funny." Zach pulsed a cynical smile. "He's saying I need to make sure I'm doing something that really matters with my life. He's never been a big fan of my drawings or architecture or the big commercial buildings your dad's team builds. And especially all the money we've made."

"Oh, come on!" Mags retorted.

Zach continued. "Several years ago, he informed me, rather judgmentally, that I had already made two or three times more money in my three short decades than he's made across his almost fifty years. Then he said, 'You know, there's more to life than building fancy buildings and making a pile of cash. Remember, it's all going to burn up someday, Son. Your aunt and I always hoped and prayed you would become a missionary to Africa or a pastor here in the good ol' USA. People need the Lord. Make sure you're making your life count, *really* count. Save souls, Zach. Be a fisher of men.'"

Zach exhaled and then exclaimed, "Arrrrgh! This all just drives me batty inside."

"Why?" Maggie asked. "Why does it agitate you so? Do you actually think he could be right?"

Zach frowned. "That's just my dilemma. The little poem seems on target in a certain sense. Parts of it *sound* so right. Or close to right. Across the years growing up, I heard passionate camp speakers and missionaries by the boatload share their *make your life matter* themes. But that was always linked with impassioned appeal to *become a missionary* or *surrender your life to full-time church ministry.* And it was always more than implied, *You'll have to turn your back on money, success, and accomplishment, IF you're laying your all on the altar.*"

Maggie scrunched up her nose, grinned, and nodded. "I'm very familiar with such messages."

Zach continued, "Honestly, Mags, I was willing to do that, and I seriously contemplated it. But I never sensed my personal call, talents, gifts, and passions fit the missionary or pastor profile. Earlier than a lot of my friends, I figured out what I was good at doing, and I chose to train for it. The struggle is, Mags, now I'm feeling like a second-class citizen in the kingdom. I really *want* to honor Christ with my life. I give my tithes and offerings, generously, faithfully. I've done that for years. I even serve in some pretty cool ways at church on Sundays. But I still feel guilty."

Maggie interrupted. "How? Why?"

"I feel guilty for doing what I'm good at," Zach explained. "I'm not trying to brag, but I'm *really* good at doing design work. And yet I feel guilty for working at doing the very thing God wired me to do."

"And you are *very* gifted, skilled, and passionate for all of it," Mags affirmed. "If that's not a calling, I don't know what is."

"Of course, everything is extra-jumbled inside me right now with the economy in such sad shape. Like we talked about the other night coming across the PA Turnpike, job bids have slowed to a wicked crawl, our profit margin is sliding, and your dad and the other older guys are all telling me to cut corners right and left in my designs. Nobody can afford fancy-schmancy anymore.

> *"I'm left wondering,* is my life really mattering for anything anyway?—*I know, I'm a real piece of work right now."*

That makes me very frustrated. Then, Grandpa's condition has me going all inner-child, introspective." Mags smiled.

"Seriously," Zach continued, "I'm left wondering, *is my life really mattering for anything anyway?*—I know, I'm a real piece of work right now."

There was thick silence for a moment across the truck cab. What Zach left out was *why* Uncle Clyde's opinions mattered so much to him. A couple times a year, for several years when Zach was in grade school, his preacher-uncle had taken him out for breakfast and then fishing for the day. This extra expression of attention, blended with Uncle Clyde's larger-than-life stories, created a unique psychological bond. Though now Zach found so many things about his uncle were bizarre, otherworldly, and even repulsive, he could not help but care about how Uncle Clyde assessed his life's value and accomplishment.

Finally, Maggie broke the silence. "Wow, I guess according to your uncle's standards, I'm *really* a lower class Christian then."

"What do you mean?" Zach asked.

Mags replied, "I just work with smelly animals Monday through Friday—creatures who, by the way, have no *real* souls to save. And most Saturdays, I snap pictures of buildings that, according to your Uncle Clyde's thinking, are doomed to burn up, blow up, or otherwise crumble at the final apocalypse."

Mags' sarcasm was growing. "Say, which of us is guiltier? *You*, for designing the buildings? My dad and his builders for building them? Or *me* for pushing the marketing that entices people to build more of them, helping us all make more devilish money. Whew, I see why you're tormented, dear."

The sudden, tender term of endearment struck a curious chord for Zach. Her questions were both whimsical and serious, but the "dear" reference grabbed him in a deeper, more emotional place. Why would she say it? Why would she mess with his heart like this? She'd made it clear several years ago that she indeed loved him, loved him deeply . . . but like a brother. He had hoped for more, and so he had worked through his romantic disappointment. Now she called him dear. With a quick flash of personal insight, he chose to simply dismiss it. He chose to think, *Surely she meant nothing by it.*

After a few beats, Maggie broke the awkward moments of silence. "Random question. Change of subject. What's up with this truck? It's rusty, *really* ugly, and it smells musty. I don't think I've ever sat in anything quite like it. Seriously, what gives?"

"Gran'pa gives," Zach answered. "Am I lucky or what?" Their sarcasm was volleying.

"Yesterday at the hospital, after he told me he loved me and we hugged, Grandpa says in a gravelly voice, 'One more thing, young man. Here's your inheritance.' He handed me this set of keys and an envelope with the truck's title. 'Told me I'd find this back here in the tall weeds behind the pole barn. Then with a mysterious tone in his voice, he said, 'It doesn't look like much, but it came from Georgia, so the frame is solid. Clean it up. Get it running, and it will get you where you need to go.'"

"What in the world do you think he meant by that?" Mags asked incredulously. "You have your new G37, which is one sweet ride. It gets you everywhere you need to go, in amazing style. Does he have something against your driving an Infiniti? Is this one of those American-made-versus-foreign-made issues for him?"

"I don't know," Zach replied. "'Guess it's just a little more of Grandpa being old-fashioned. Maybe he and Uncle Clyde have been conspiring. You know, trying to further 'loosen the ungodly grip of material things on my soul' by giving me something that's a worthless rust bucket. Geez, I don't know. Perhaps it's to teach me contentment or some other eternal life lesson. Who knows?"

"So?" Mags grinned.

"So what?" Zach asked.

"So does it start? Have you turned the key?"

"No." Zach chuckled. "I've been strategically delaying my disappointment. Call me chicken, but I know it won't run. Plus, I think these old vehicles start different than new ones. 'Have to pump the gas pedal and talk nice to it and then turn the key.'"

"OK, so do it." Mags coaxed.

Zach grinned. "OK, but if we're going to talk to the truck, it needs a name. What should we call him?"

She paused and then suddenly sported a very big grin. "Henry. You know, Henry. Like Henry Ford." Mags reached across the bench, shoved Zach's shoulder playfully and laughed at her own wit. Zach shoved back.

"OK, Henry he is. Here goes. Come on, Henry, you can do it!" Five big pumps on the gas pedal. He turned the key, and to their utter amazement, "Vroooom!" Henry roared to life. Like teenagers on a winning ball team, they shouted a victorious cheer and gave each other fist pounds.

Zach quickly jammed the gear selector into drive. Suddenly, the F-100 lunged forward. The transmission slipped, but then grabbed a random gear. As if enlivened with a mind of its own, Henry accelerated across the field. And it kept gathering speed.

Having performed no preliminary mechanical checks, Zach had no way of knowing the steering fluid was too low to steer it, or that the gas pedal would stick, or that a brake line had rusted through. The primer-gray, rust-spotted pickup was on its way, carrying Mags and Zach somewhere they had never been, a spot they would have never imagined, and a place they never would have chosen to go all on their own.

Reflecting on Henry's Story, God's Story, and Your Story

1. Can you relate at all to Zach's inner turmoil? Regarding your own work, do you ever wonder, *How much of this, if any of this, really matters anyway? Should I remain in this field? I love what I do, but is it really what I'm supposed to be doing with my life?*

2. Why is Zach so bothered by Uncle Clyde's poetry recitation and perspective? What do you find bothersome and problematic about it? Why? Have you ever encountered this perspective in your own life and experiences?

3. Zach shares with Maggie his frustration with the tight economy, sliding profits, and his boss and coworkers' attempts to cut some ethical corners. Where and when have you experienced similar frustrations in your workplace? How have you handled economic and ethical pressures?

4. Uncle Clyde projects a "money and profit are evil" mindset on Zach and Maggie. Do you agree? Why or why not? How do you respond to this mindset?

5. Explore God's foundational example as the Creative Ruler and Worker in Genesis chapter 1. Make a list of what you learn about his work approach from his opening chapter in his story. What stand out to you as God's attitudes and actions at work?

6. Take these three initial action steps in prayer. (1) Ask God to show you more of his perspective on life and work in the chapters to come. (2) Ask God to show you how he is already at work in your daily life and in the lives of people you interact with at work every day. (3) Ask God to help you sense one to three people in or through your daily workplace who need to encounter Christ.

CHAPTER TWO

Mission to Marshall

BAM! Crunch! Henry, the mind-of-his-own Ford F-100, slammed into the fence. Shpooshhhhh. Steam spewed from under the hood into the dark night sky. There was nothing but moonlight and more fireflies.

Henry's speed had been slowed by the tall corn and the gradual uphill climb right before he came to an abrupt stop. He embedded his steel bumper into the old fence, landing three neighbors and only about twenty-five acres away from Zach's grandparents' house.

"Whoa! What in the world?! Never saw that coming. Are you OK?" Zach reached for Maggie's arm, and she instinctively pulled closer to him.

"I'm fine," she said as she quietly exhaled. "Just glad we got stopped. It all happened so fast. Where are we?"

"I'm not exactly sure," Zach replied. "Too dark to really tell, but I think we launched through the edge of the neighbor's field. Since we took out some rows of corn and some boards of fence, I'm afraid we're going to have to meet this neighbor tomorrow." They climbed out of Henry and found him still all in one piece, only a slight bend in the front bumper.

"I guess it's true," Mags offered as they walked their way up the road. "They don't make 'em like they used to. Most of today's cars would be crumpled if they kissed that fence. And hey, at least we know it runs." Maggie had a way of always trying to find the bright side, even on a dark night.

Zach rolled his eyes. "Yea, it runs—just enough to be dangerous, expensive and complicated." Zach shook his head in dismay. "Nothing is ever easy, is it? It's the story of my life, or so it seems. If you can't tell, I'm just a little underwhelmed by my inheritance from Grandpa."

The next morning, Zach rolled out of bed around 7:15. Grandma was already eating a bagel and sipping coffee on the back patio. Her call to the hospital at 6:30 a.m. had revealed that Grandpa successfully made it through another night. In fact, his vitals were actually stronger this morning than they had been the morning before.

"Praise God!" Grandma exclaimed. "Looks like several of us can stop in to see him in a little bit!" She was obviously encouraged by the nurse's rather optimistic report.

"Can we wait an hour or so?" Zach asked. "I can't go until I walk up the road and explain to the neighbor about the truck and fence." Then he muttered under his breath as if Grandma might not hear him. "That rickety bundle of bolts is proving to be such a nuisance." She just grinned.

"Well, if my memory serves me correctly," Gram was pondering, "if it's the field and fence I think you're describing, I believe that's Marshall's property. He and your grandpa have worked on stuff across the years together. Marshall Scott. That's his name. You'll probably find him pleasant enough to talk to. If indeed that's the field you landed in, get ready. Brace yourself for a pretty big talkin' session. Your grandpa has always said that Marshall's a real talker." Grandma smiled an ornery smile and poured Zach some coffee.

After eggs and java, Zach headed out the door. He got halfway down the lane and suddenly heard, "Hey, wait for me!" Mags was up. She'd thrown on jeans and a sweatshirt, tossed her hair in a headband, and dashed out front after Zach.

"Wait up!" Mags called. "I overheard Grandma telling you about the neighbor, Marshall. I gotta meet him and see the truck and fence damage now in the daylight."

Walking back a long country lane, the two timidly stepped onto the expansive porch that stretched the front and wrapped 'round two other sides of the farmhouse. There was an old swing dangling from well-worn, rusty chains and a couple classic wicker chairs. They knocked. No answer. They knocked again. Still no answer.

They stepped off the porch and were about to head back out the lane, when they heard a strangely familiar sound. It was the vroom-hum of Henry's motor. To their sudden shock, there was the F-100, coming down the lane. He was being driven by a round-faced, jolly-looking gentlemen, puffing on a pipe.

"Mornin'!" Marshall shouted overtop the loud exhaust. "I'm guessin' this creature must belong to you." The Ford came to a noisy stop as the brakes made a great grinding sound. "I think I have the other issues ironed out, at least for now. And we can work on those brakes some afternoon this week." He was shouting, smiling, and exuding a tool man confidence.

Zach extended an awkward handshake and curiously introduced himself. "Um, geez, thanks. I don't understand. We were just coming to explain what happened and tell you how we'd work to get this old clunker off your property and help fix your fence before the week is over. How in the world did you already make it run again? I'm honestly a bit floored."

Marshall chuckled out a hearty laugh, and he turned the key to shut it down. His belly shook and rings of sweet-smelling smoke ascended into the air from his pipe. "Well, I heard the commotion through the corn 'bout half past ten last night, and I could even see lights bobbing through the stalks as I sat up there on the front porch in the dark. First I thought you must be a bunch of teens out carousin', but then I saw you two step out of the field and wander up the road. I figured you'd be back to claim your prized possession."

He stepped from the truck cab and continued explaining. "This mornin', I got up early and had to go explorin'. Sure enough, I recognized the truck. Your gran'pa showed it to me several years ago after he purchased it from down south. 'Said he would resell it on his car lot and probably make some good profit, based on its re-con potential. I'm a Ford lover, ever since I was a kid. I've owned at least ten of my own over the years. I've lost count. And I've worked on dozens more for other folks."

"Wow, so you knew exactly what this thing needed done to make it run?" Zach said with an incredulous tone.

"Yes, and if you'd like, I can help you with a handful of other simple things that will get it more roadworthy."

"Gee, that would be great. Thanks *so* much. I'm an architect. Not a mechanic. I know just enough to be dangerous when it comes to working on cars. Whenever I've tried to work on my own vehicle or help Grandpa, I've ended up with parts left over."

Marshall laughed again, as did Maggie, and then Zach asked, "So, I'm just wondering. Why in the world would you help us like this? You hadn't even met us yet."

"Wellll," Marshall replied with a drawl, "come on up and sit a spell on my porch. Let's get outta this hot mornin' sun." Zach thought to himself, *Oh boy, Grandma warned me that he's a talker.*

"Grandma said you know my grandpa pretty well," Zach began.

"Sure do. In fact, I really owe my whole life and work to two fellas. First, to Jesus. And then your gran'pa is the other. Sincerely, I owe my life to him."

"What do you mean?" Zach was extremely curious about this mysterious man from his grandfather's past, and such a bold claim about his grandfather. "Grandpa never told me about any heroic life rescues that I can remember."

Marshall cleared his throat, stumped the ashes from his pipe, and began to explain.

"About ten years ago, my life was wrecked and broken down bad. I was living only for me. I hated my life, 'specially being a mechanic. It seemed like such a pointless job, just workin' for grumpy people on broken-down vehicles, only to have 'em break down again. Sure, I had a real knack for fixin' things, but I felt ashamed to be one of those grease monkeys. Might sound goofy, but my whole life felt very hollow. Worse yet, I was angry, and hurtin' my wife, and I didn't realize it. I was drinkin' way too much in the evenin's and on the weekends. Guess you could say, I was living only for Marshall

Scott." He paused long enough to relight his pipe and take a couple puffs.

"Humph," Marshall continued through a profound snort. "You think your F-100 has troubles. My life was brok'n down, busted and dented. Seemed *way* beyond repair. Kay was threatenin' to leave me if things didn't change."

> "We kept eatin' breakfasts and talkin'. Pretty simple, really. Over about two years, he listened to me, and told me more and more 'bout Jesus' life, and grace, and His great big love for me. Eventually, I gave my life to Christ."

"Sounds like it was a real bad spot in life for you," Zach offered.

"Sure was," Marshall continued. "'Bout that time, I met your gran'pa. I had lived here in this place for many years, but had never yet met your gran'folks. So one day, your gran'pa had some other Ford that wasn't runnin' right, some old Taurus he was tryin' to sell up on his used car lot. Someone in town told him 'bout me. They called me 'that guy three doors down with the small cornfield, who works on Fords.' So we met, and he had me do some work for him. After I finished that job and he paid me, he asked me if I wanted to do breakfast together on Saturday. That got us started eatin' breakfast together at the Buckeye Lake Truck Stop two or three times a month.

"Yep, breakfast out. Gran'pa loves to eat breakfast out," Zach commented.

"Sure does," Marshall replied. "A couple weeks after I worked on that Ford for him, he did some welding work for me in his pole barn, and the work just kind of swapped back and forth 'tween us 'cross these years. All along the way, your grandpa was kind and honest, hard-workin' and fair-payin'. I could tell that somethin' was different 'bout him, so the closer we got over breakfasts, well, the more I started sharin' with him and askin' him questions. We kept eatin' breakfasts and talkin'. Pretty simple, really. Over about two years, he listened to me, and told me more and more 'bout Jesus' life, and grace, and God's great big love for me. Eventually, I gave my life to Christ."

By now, Marshall's eyes were leaking profusely. He pulled a big old red hanky from his overalls. Maggie and Zach were glued to his every word.

"Your grandpa and I kept workin' on car projects together and workin' on my growin' to know Jesus better and better. It was truly amazin'. I got to know Jesus, both in the Good Book and my everyday life. And my actions started changin' with the work of the Lord in me. Yep, I tell folks, he did one great big engine overhaul, a mighty big work in my life."

There was a silent pause. Marshall was choking through his tears. "And your grandpa worked with Jesus and his Spirit, so that overhaul could happen. I became a better husband and dad. And over time, I even became a better Ford repair guy, because of Jesus' work in my life. But I think that's another story for another time. I gotta let you kids get goin'. I've kept you too long, and I'm sure you got places to go today."

"Wow!" Zach expressed. "Thanks for sharing, Marshall. Grandma did say she wanted to head to the hospital to see Grampa. The nurses said he was doing pretty well this morning."

Marshall grinned. "Your grandpa's always been a stubborn old cuss. I reckon he's not fixin' to go home until the good Lord fin'ly calls him."

Now it was Mags and Zach chuckling. "Yup, you *do* know Grandpa."

They climbed into Henry. With five pumps of the gas pedal and a turn of the key, he started right up.

"Do you think he'll get us up the road to Gram's?" Maggie asked.

Marshall was choking through his tears. "And your grandpa worked with Jesus and his Spirit, so that overhaul could happen. I became a better husband and dad. And over time, I even became a better Ford repair guy, because of Jesus' work in my life."

"Do I think? I *know* he will. In fact, if he was tagged, you could drive him over to the hospital. But no registration yet, and we probably should do those brakes, just to be safe. 'Don't need you two kids runnin' into any other folks' corn and fences." Marshall winked. "Bring him back over, maybe Wednesday or Thursday, and we'll do some more fixin' work on the old fella."

Zach replied, "Great. Thanks *so* much, Marshall. We'll be back over. And please figure up what we owe you for the repairs. We'll settle up. Catch you soon!"

Marshall gave a wave as they headed out his driveway and back to Gram's.

Reflecting on Henry's Story, God's Story, and Your Story

1. What impresses you about Marshall's attitude and actions in helping fix Henry? What seems to be his motivation?

2. Analyze Zach's grandfather's outlook and actions toward Marshall through their business interaction. How was Grandpa involved in a missional sense?

3. Marshall realizes, in retrospect, that Grandpa was actually *working with God.*

   Read these passages in God's story: John 5:16–20 and John 15:4–5.

   What insights does Jesus convey? What do you learn about working with God?

How might this change your own outlook or others' outlook on work?

4. Identify one to three people in or through your workplace (coworkers, clients, or other business contacts) whom you sense need to encounter Christ. Begin praying for them each day. Watch for multiple opportunities to get to know them better. Keep your conversation light, fun, and "normal." After each opportunity, take some notes. Write down what you learned about their lives. Continue praying for them in light of what you are learning about them and ask God to help you cultivate these relationships.

CHAPTER THREE

Highs & Lows

Mid-morning, Grandpa was actually sitting up when they rapped on his door and peaked in. He flashed a smile as Zach, Grandma, and Maggie entered the room.

"Hi, Grampa. How are you?" Zach asked.

"I'm having a pretty good morning. Nurses say my vitals are strong, and they commented that I'm more ornery than normal. I think this is a good sign."

"Good, indeed, but no flirting or chasing nurses," Grandma chided him.

"You'll never believe what we've been up to and who we met, Grampa." Zach and Maggie excitedly recounted their adventures with run-away Henry and their new friend, Marshall Scott.

Grandpa gave them a whimsical grin and crooked his eyebrow. "That Marshall was a real piece of work when I met him. Everything he told you about his old life being all broken down is true, and then some. But we just kept doing breakfast at the truck stop, and eventually, God's work in him was very effective and powerful. I'll never forget the day he said, 'Phil, last night I did it. I gave my heart to Jesus. I feel very different this mornin', though I can't quite splain it." Grandpa paused, his eyes now filled with tears.

He continued through a sniffle and a wipe of his cheeks. "In months to follow, Marshall introduced me to a bunch of other Ford guys and trucker friends he worked with over the years. Marsh and I just kept doing breakfast with guys, listening to their stories, praying for them, and sharing Jesus. Over the years, several more of our friends who were grease monkeys and truckers became Jesus-followers. It's been *very, very* good." More tears flowed. Gram squeezed Grandpa's hand and helped wipe the tears away.

"That's amazing, Grampa," Zach reflected. "How's that happen? Seriously. How does a guy go from despising his life, drinking too much, verbally abusing his wife, and hating his work, to actually helping other guys meet Jesus?"

Grandpa smiled again, took a big breath, and Grandma helped reposition his pillow behind his back.

"Well, after Marshall gave his life to Christ, he started growing and changing. I mean really changing, a step at a time. One of the biggest ways he was changing was he started realizing God's call, God's unique purpose for his life. He started to believe down deep that we're really here to serve other people, for the glory of God. In fact, we talked about this truth that everything we do, it should be our goal to do it for the glory of God. The Apostle Paul, in Colossians 3:23–24, said, 'Whatever you do, work at it with all your heart, as working for the Lord, not for human masters, since you know that you will receive an inheritance from the Lord as a reward. It is the Lord Christ you are serving.' And we also talked a bunch about Paul's words in 1 Corinthians 10:31, 'So whether you eat or drink or whatever you do, do it all for the glory of God.' Marsh started to realize that even fixing Fords can be done to serve others, to the glory of God."

> *He started to believe down deep that we're really here to serve other people, for the glory of God. In fact, we talked about this truth that everything we do, it should be our goal to do it for the glory of God.*

Maggie jumped in: "No wonder he was so quick to grab his tools and fix Henry this morning." She had a quick mind for correlating with everyday life.

"No surprise to me." Grandpa was shaking his head. "He saw that as serving you and bringing God glory. Every little thing, or big thing, *can* be and *should* be done to the glory of God. So, instead of his wrenching and fix-time on a Ford just being 'grease monkey' work, he learned he could actually bless others, bless the Lord, and help advance his kingdom. More than once over the past ten years, Marshall has said, 'Phil, my mission field is fixin' Fords and hangin' 'round the truck stop with these truckers. The more I work my mission field, the more I see God a-workin' in other guys' lives. I love it.'"

Zach said nothing, but he was thinking deep. His synapses were firing fast, trying to consider the implications for his own architectural work back in Valley Forge. So much of this smacked of his Uncle Clyde's lingo about saving souls, reaching people for eternity. But there was something deeper, something richer, and more robust underneath all of this. Zach thought, *Something about Grandpa's approach seems real, deep-down genuine, somehow more like what I imagine Jesus' own approach to be with people.* Numerous questions were buzzing in Zach's heart and mind.

Just then, there was another knock on the hospital room door. Grandpa glanced that way to see a familiar face.

"G'morning, come on in, Benny," Grandpa greeted him with an extra dose of excitement. "'Want you to meet some of my family. You already know Claire."

"Of course, who doesn't know Claire?" Ben replied. Everyone chuckled.

"So this is my oldest grandson, Zach, and his very special friend, Maggie Brinkley." Both Zach and Mags blushed a bit at his reference to Mags as *his very special friend.*

"Kids, this is Dr. Benjamin Clinton. Benny's been a chaplain here at the hospital ever since he retired from teaching and chaplaincy over at the University several years back. Should they call you Dr. Ben?"

"No, no. Just Ben will do." The slender-framed, gray-goateed, balding friend waved off the title with an air of insistence.

Maggie smiled big. "We *must* call you Doc Ben. We both loved our college years and our college profs and the rich learning experiences, both in and out of the classroom. *Please* allow us to call you Doc." There was a hint of pleading in her voice.

Ben acquiesced. "OK, but only because you insist." Actually, your grandpa and I have known each other for a bunch of years. Gone to men's groups together at church and drank lots of coffee together. He even got me to come out to the truck stop several times."

"That's right," Grandpa chimed in. "Lots of coffee. I was just talking to them about what you taught me years ago, about working to serve others, for God's glory and advancing his kingdom. I was telling them about Marshall Scott. Remember Marshall?"

"Absolutely. I most certainly do." Ben gave a chuckle and shook, a motion that distinctly smacked of playful imitation. Everyone played along with their own Marshall-like chuckles.

"Yes, those biblical concepts, directly from Saint Paul's teaching were revolutionary for Marshall," Doc Ben explained. "'Remarkably changed his perspective on *who* he works for and *why* he works every day.'"

"We saw that in living color just a few hours ago," Zach interjected. "It was as if he totally delighted in fixing the old F-100, like he knew he was *made* for doing exactly that work, and as if all heaven *smiled* when he did it. What's amazing to me is how few people I've ever met who actually see their work this way, you know, truly confident of their calling. Growing up, I mostly got the idea that God is impressed with Sunday stuff—you know, worship music, Sunday School lessons, and certainly my Uncle Clyde's sermons." Zach rolled his eyes as he said it.

> *"Growing up, I mostly got the idea that God is impressed with Sunday stuff—you know, worship music, Sunday School lessons, and certainly my Uncle Clyde's sermons." Zach rolled his eyes as he said it.*

Zach was on a roll and he continued. "Anybody who works on these activities on Sundays, well, they are doing God's *real* work, the truly *sacred* stuff. Oh, and you can throw missionaries into the 'approved & sacred' list of workers as well. Their overseas missions, this kind of work also qualifies for the A-list, the smile-of-God work. But everything else, well, not so much. All the rest of us workers who do ordinary work on Mondays through Saturdays, ours is just *secular* work. At best, we make God's B or C list, *if* and it's a big IF, we tithe on our income to support more of that *real*, sacred work that happens on Sundays and in Africa."

Doc Ben was snickering with sincerity now. Grandpa Phil was sporting a rye, knowing nod and pinching the end of his nose.

"What? What am I saying that you two find so amusing? That's just what I grew up sensing, feeling, and thinking." Zach was mildly defensive.

"I know. I know," Grandpa kept nodding. "That outlook is everywhere. In fact, I was a primary proponent of such split-life thinking for a large portion of my life." He started to cough and reached for his water cup. Gram helped him.

Sipping through his straw, Grandpa continued. "Benny here can tell you the full history on where this thinking comes from, but it's sure not new." Ben was nodding. Grandpa coughed again and motioned for Ben to take over.

"Your grandfather is exactly right," Ben chimed in. "The seeds of such thinking were planted through ancient Greek philosophy, Plato in fact. He taught there was a higher realm, and there was a lower realm. Spiritual and mental pursuits were higher, whereas earthly, physical things were lower. Guess where human work fell on the scale."

Mags jumped in, "Low, of course."

"Ding-ding-ding. You win the prize," Doc Ben congratulated. "During the fifth century AD, the early church father, Augustine, adopted and synchronized such thinking into church theology. Across the decades to come, this thinking helped create a sacred-secular divide, resulting in a sharp distinction between the contemplative life and the active life. En masse, people espoused a divided way of living instead of an integrated, holistic approach. And the same perspective spilled over into people's views of work and workers. So now today, most people think of secular roles and sacred roles. There are the ordinary workers and the more sacred ones, like pastors and missionaries."

"Well-said, Benny," Grandpa rejoined with explanation. "For me, I thought of Sundays and all mission and church activities as the high and mighty, grandly spiritual, God-approved stuff, and all the rest of work and life outside of Sunday church was *lower, less-than-spiritual,* and certainly not able to have eternal, lasting kingdom impact. Everything you just said, Zach, I believed and I behaved in light of it. It wasn't until Ben started working me over about ten years ago that I began to gradually think and behave in different ways. In fact, I now realize, I never could have had the impact on Marshall and other truck guys, were it not for such a big change in my perspective."

Just then, the room door flew open and in marched three nurses. "OK, folks, sounds like you're having fun. Sorry to spoil the party, but we need some quality time with Mr. Popularity here." They proceeded to explain that it was time for a fresh round of blood work and a check of Grandpa's vitals.

"So, out we go, kids." Grandma motioned for the door. "It's already past noon, and we can come back later this evening. Let 'em work and then Grandpa can get some rest."

"I need to scoot too," Ben said with a tone of disappointment. "And we were just getting rolling on the good stuff."

Grandpa raised his hand in the air for a moment and pointed his finger, as if he was issuing an emperor's decree. "Here's what you three need to do." Everyone paused. He had their attention. "Promise me that you will go for coffee together in this next week, whether I'm still here or gone to glory. Promise me. And keep this conversation about work and the kingdom going. I sense you're really going somewhere with this. Don't miss this, Zach. It's very important. Don't miss it."

"Got it," Zach assured. "I won't. I promise, Grandpa." Everyone pushed back some tears, shared hugs, and told him 'I love you' before turning for the door. They all sensed the deep and lively conversation had nearly worn him out. He settled back, took a big deep breath, and relaxed into his pillow as the nurses started their work.

Just as they all turned to leave, Grandpa suddenly sat up again and spoke with fresh fervor. "One more thing, Grandson. Get those brakes fixed before the week is out, and don't think for a second that falls in the lower category. Very high and sacred." Everyone laughed in admiration at his still-strong sense of humor. "Go see Marshall." Grandpa continued, but now very serious. "You're going to need that truck to go back to Pennsylvania."

Honestly, taking Henry on an eight-hour road trip was about the furthest thing from Zach's mind, in light of the Ford's age and seemed worn-out condition. *No way it would make it,* Zach processed to himself. *Not even sure I'm going to keep the old beast.*

But he just smiled and nodded. "Thanks, Grandpa. 'Love you."

Down in the hospital parking lot, Doc Ben gave Zach his mobile number.

Zach was very receptive. "It would be great to get together, just like my grandfather said. I've got a lot of thoughts spinning right now. Our conversation back there in his room gives me a lot to consider. Honestly, I'm very conflicted right now about work, my calling, and God's overall purpose for my life. I guess I just have a bunch of questions and ideas that chase through the halls of my mind." Zach ran his fingers back through his wavy hair. Maggie grinned. She had learned across the years that motion meant he was very serious in all he was contemplating.

"Sounds good to me," Ben replied. "How 'bout tomorrow morning for coffee, say 8:00 a.m. at Dunkin' Donuts? I need to make visitation rounds back here about ten o'clock. That should give us some time to pick up where we left off, plus talk on a couple related topics."

Zach ran his fingers back through his wavy hair. Maggie grinned. She had learned across the years that motion meant he was very serious in all he was contemplating.

After dinner, Zach spent most of the evening doing something he'd never have dreamed of doing just a couple days ago. He got busy vacuuming the carpet and dusting cobwebs and crumbs out of the F-100. He even got out the garden hose and sprayed grimy leaves out of the pickup bed. Then he stepped back to examine Henry's profile. The old F-100 seemed to already look a bit brighter. He even appeared to be sporting a smile through his round headlight eyes and wide-mouth bumper.

This thing means so much to Grampa and Marshall, Zach mused. *I guess the least I can do is spiff it up a bit. God knows I can't actually do anything mechanical on it.* And he kept working until it was too dark to see what he was cleaning. Little did he realize, the old, primer gray, rust-spotted vehicle that seemed like nothing but a nuisance just three days ago was casting a captivating spell over the young east coast architect's imagination. And he could have never fully imagined the higher places Henry would take him in the days to come.

Reflecting on Henry's Story, God's Story, and Your Story

1. Grandpa told Zach and Maggie, "We just kept doing breakfast at the truck stop, and eventually, God's work in him was very effective and powerful." What do you learn from Grandpa's approach with Marshall?

2. Explore Colossians 3:23–24 and 1 Corinthians 10:31. What are the implications from these truths for your everyday workplace endeavors?

3. Analyze the sacred-secular divide that Doc Ben describes. When have you personally, or others around you, been living life like this? What's the problem with this perspective?

4. Right now, would you say you are living a compartmentalized life or an integrated life? Explain why.

5. Grandpa said that as Marshall was growing in Christ, he "started realizing God's call, God's unique purpose for his life. He started to believe down deep that we're really here to serve other people, for the glory of God . . . everything we do, it should be our goal to do it for the glory of God."

   Do you agree? Would you say this is true of your outlook and sense of calling right now? Why or why not? How can you develop a clearer sense of call?

6. Take the action step of inviting one of those coworkers, clients, or other business contacts (from those whom you've been praying for) to do breakfast, lunch, or coffee with you in the next week. Enjoy the conversation. Hear some of his/her story. Get to know each other better. Afterward, add notes about what you learned and continue to pray for this person in light of the specifics you learned about her/his life situations.

CHAPTER FOUR

Coffee & Creation

The sun was up, and so was Grandma. An early shaft of light streamed in his back bedroom window. Zach could smell coffee brewing as he rolled out. Grandpa had another good night, and the nurse on shift reported he was "in good spirits, ornery as ever." Suddenly, Zach realized it was already 7:15.

"Sorry, no time for eggs, Gram. I need to get ready and scoot. I'm supposed to meet Doc Ben at Dunkin's around 8:00. Can you go wake up Maggie? I think she's on the living room couch. I'm sure she wants to go with me."

Grandma raised her eyebrows. "I'm *sure* she does." Zach smiled and ran to get ready.

When they arrived at Dunkin's, Ben was already seated in the corner at the large, harvest orange, round table. "Hello, friends!" Ben stood up for handshakes and hugs. Based on the spread of books, leather journal, and coffee-stained napkins, Zach and Mags could safely conclude he had already been working for a couple hours. The professor's well-worn corduroy jacket bore further evidence of his morning indulgence. Chocolate chip muffin crumbs. Of course, he insisted on buying Zach and Maggie coffees and muffins.

"So any word on your grandfather this morning?" Ben asked.

Zach gave him the encouraging report.

"Very good," Doc replied. "I'll be sure to stop by to see him when I get in later. So, let's dive back in where we left off. What have you been thinking since our talk yesterday? We were wrestling with the whole perspectives issue of sacred vs. secular, higher vs. lower, spiritual vs. ordinary when it comes to work. Any more thoughts?"

Maggie jumped right in. "Well, I work with animals. I run a vet clinic, and I *never* thought about my work like that before—the whole idea of my Monday through Friday meaning something to God's kingdom. I'm still trying to grasp that. I just love animals. 'Seems I always have. To be honest, I like animals a heck of a lot more than I like their owners. Most pet owners are rather annoying, stupid, and not nearly as wonderful as their fine furry friends."

Doc Ben started laughing, "Well, dear Maggie, you'll be happy to know that your work has some doggone great meaning. No pun intended."

Mags grinned. She thought, *I'm liking this guy's quirky sense of humor.*

He continued: "You see, what you do is *so* deeply original to what God intended for humans to be all about. I get goose bumps just thinking about how close you are to the heart of God."

Zach interjected. "What do you mean?" His voice held a skeptical tone.

Ben started nodding, took a giant gulp of his mocha, and opened his iPad.

He lowered his voice, as if he was about to reveal a deep, dark secret. "All of God's story and his intended glory for humanity, past, present, and future, come to life from these words."

"Look at this. First chapter of Genesis in the Bible, verses 26–28. After everything else had been created, then God created the first man and woman. And he declared they were created in his image. Scholars call this the *imago Dei*, the image of God. And he goes on to explain who they are and what their purpose is to be. It says, 'God blessed them and said to them, 'Be fruitful and increase in number; fill the earth and subdue it. Rule over the fish in the seas and the birds in the sky and over every living creature that moves on the ground.' He commanded them to rule over *every living creature.*"

A funny smile came over Mags' face. "Wow. I've heard the Creation story before, but I never thought of my vet business as matching up like that. 'Makes perfect sense." She shook her head with amazement at such affirming correlation for her veterinary work.

"Yes, yes, very good," Ben affirmed. "But there's so much more right here. These dusty old lines of sacred text are mysteriously foundational for all of our purpose and potential for heart-and-soul work as people made in God's image." He lowered his voice, as if he was about to reveal a deep, dark secret. "All of God's story and his intended glory for humanity, past, present, and future, come to life from these words."

Zach and Maggie's eyes widened, and they instinctively put down their coffees and leaned in closer. Ben paused, realized he had captured these bright kids' attention, and he took the next cerebral jump into the deep end of the pool.

"Words, several old words give us the clues. Let's name just a handful. *Blessed.* That one is going to come out over and over again in God's grand story throughout the Bible. We better watch for it. *Be fruitful and multiply, fill the earth and subdue it. And rule over* . . . There's so much more wrapped up in these ideas than just making babies to increase the world population."

Zach and Mags chuckled and blushed a bit at the professor's candid wit. He continued, "The whole scene speaks of creating and ruling like a king, exercising bold, strategic leadership over the earth. Genesis 1 reveals God as the King, the Creator and Master-Worker. Made in his image, we are commissioned to be co-creators and coworkers in his kingdom. The language of king and kingdom is woven across the whole rest of the story, all the way to the wrap-up in the New Testament book of Revelation."

Doc Ben paused briefly. "There's more. Most Bible scholars believe chapter 2 of Genesis supplies a re-telling of the creation of humans, only now with greater specifics. Another big word clue is laying in the dust right here in Genesis 2, verse 15. God put the man in the Garden of Eden "to *work* it and take care of it." The word for *work* also gets repeated all over the grand story in the Bible.

Sometimes, it's translated as *work* and other times as *serve*. In so many places, it's the same word."

Doc paused, and then emphatically reflected, "Personally, I find it *amazing* that it's translated both ways throughout the Bible. The idea proves stunningly pivotal midway through the grand story. The prophet Isaiah foretells the coming of the Messiah and calls him the *servant* or *worker* of the Lord. 'Same old root word there in Isaiah 42 as back in Genesis 2. And then when Jesus comes, Matthew reports in his gospel, chapter 12 and verses eighteen through twenty-one, how Jesus proclaims and performs compassionate acts of service. In so doing, he proved he was the fulfillment of that ancient prophecy in Isaiah 42."

Ben quickly scrolled there on his iPad and read it to them. With excitement, he dove deeper. "Later on, in his letter to the Philippians, chapter 2, Saint Paul calls the Philippian believers, and by echo of application, all of us as Christ-followers today, to have the same attitude of mind as Christ Jesus. We are to have the outlook and actions of a Christ-like slave, a servant-worker . . . *to the glory of God the Father.*"

> *"I believe that when people glorify God, they are spotlighting him, making him famous to others, helping other people encounter his character, his attitude, and actions in saving, redeeming, hope-filled ways."*

Ben realized he was diving very deep at a rapid pace, so he paused, as if to come up for air. He smiled. "You kids still with me?"

Mags and Zach shifted in their chairs, stretched, and took sips of coffee. Zach nodded. "I think I'm with you, but I'm wondering. You said, 'several old words give us the clues.' So, this *glory* word. It keeps coming up. I've heard it thrown around over the years. What's it mean, really? Please enlighten us."

"Great question!" Doc Ben affirmed. "Glory's old Hebrew root word is the idea of something being heavy, weighty, honorable, and impressive. Psalm 24, verses seven through ten, describe God as the king of glory who has done glorious deeds. Throughout the Bible, glory is often connected to shining light, like the glory of the LORD as he appeared to Moses in Exodus 33 and 34. Moses' face took on the radiance of the LORD's glory. The glory of the LORD shined all around the shepherds the night of Jesus' birth in Luke 2. There is often an accompanying radiating brilliance. So, glory is this idea of something or someone, and most remarkably God himself, being impressive, radiant, and reflecting highest honor."

"That's thoughtful and helpful," Zach responded, "but what's it mean to say that we *glorify* him?"

"Another *great* question!" Doc Ben grinned with approval. "Here is that concept that in our co-creating and co-ruling, we are helping make him famous, spotlighting his powerful character and empowering presence through our words and actions. Here's that awesome role we get to play in and through our good works. Other people can be influenced and encounter his impressive honor. I believe that when people glorify God, they are spotlighting him, making him famous to others, helping other people encounter his character, his attitude, and actions in saving, redeeming, hope-filled ways."

"Very cool," Zach exclaimed.

"And there's one more layer of understanding I want to high-light," Doc added. "*Glory* becomes a descriptor label for the entirety of what's to come with Christ's future kingdom—the new heavens and new earth. All of the redemption that people can yet anticipate. That's the *glory* to come."

"Fascinating," Zach reflected. "So much wrapped up in one little word we so often throw around."

"True, very true," Ben affirmed.

Zach continued, "So, I'm sensing some big implications. But let me get this straight. God's original intention for us, made in his image, was that *we* would be creative workers, servants and king-like rulers, alongside him?" It was both a question and a clarifying statement.

"Absolutely." Doc affirmed. "And there's more."

"I'm getting the idea there's still *a lot* more to the story," Maggie quipped. "Just a few things I didn't quite catch in Sunday School."

Ben was laughing and nodding. "Yes, it's always been there in the story. We've heard it read. But most of us have missed the deeper nuances and the important impact for our daily work as God's coworkers, the way God originally designed us."

"Yes, but it's hitting me." Zach became animated. "There is something very off-whack for us now. Not only have we missed these words in the story, we're *so* far from living this story in our daily lives. So many of us lack a sense that our work really matters or makes any difference. Many people hate their jobs. A bunch of folks spend most of their lives questioning if they're doing the right job. And many people who do seem to thrive, well, honestly, they seem to just be on an ego rush or a money trip. Most workers do not think of God, faith, ethics, and spirituality as having any practical bearing on their work life. I don't think I'm stretching things to say that very few of us feel like we play an important, kingly role in God's story, for his glory. We certainly don't come close to tasting the glory, that *image* thing. What did you call that?"

Doc Ben and Mags both laughed. "I know!" Mags announced with some healthy pride. "I learned a little Latin in a cultures class during college. It's *imago Dei.*"

"You're exactly right, both of you. Right on in your pronunciation, Miss Maggie, and frighteningly accurate in your assessment of the majority of everyday workers, Doc Zach." Zach smiled at the doctoral affirmation coming his way.

"And do you have any clue *why* most people feel this way about their work?" Ben asked his two young scholars. They shook their heads with blank stares. "I'll give you a clue," he quickly responded. "The next chapter in God's story, do you remember what happens?"

Maggie spoke up. "Genesis 3. I think that's where Adam and Eve eat the forbidden fruit. Am I right?" Zach started nodding in agreement.

Doc Ben proceeded. "Yes, and one of the strands in the tangled knot of sin's curse is the rascally impact on humanity's work. What previously had been full of meaning, carrying a real sense of purpose, joyful creativity, and fulfillment in serving, is now plagued with trouble, struggle, added sweat, and even relational turmoil."

"So let me get this straight," Zach said. "I grew up thinking that we have to work as a result of sin. Instead, work was originally intended as a very good thing, but it got spoiled in humanity's sinful fall?" Ben was nodding. "That's different from the way I've thought about work in the past," Zach clarified. "This means, if I'm hearing this correctly, that God originally intended for our work to be full of purpose, joy, real productivity. And when work is not that way, well, it's a big ugly reminder of the painful consequences of our sin."

"Absolutely!" Ben affirmed. "And it reminds us in big ways of why Jesus came. Scholars call this the *missio Dei*. The mission of God." Maggie repeated it, practicing her new Latin aloud, and Doc Ben smiled with approval.

Zach rolled his eyes. "You always were the teacher's pet."

"You're just jealous I know some Latin," Mags beamed. "You'll get over it."

Ben continued with a grin. "God's grand story hinges on his missional plans to redeem humans *and* all creation. Paul explodes that concept in Romans 8 when he talks about the Spirit giving people new life. And he proceeds to explain that all of creation is groaning in anticipation of what is yet to come with future glory. Jesus is that promised Redeemer, and I believe a great big part of the creation he came to redeem is *our work*. After all, such work was a big part of the original grand plans and good purposes at the start of the story with Creation."

> "Jesus is that promised Redeemer, and I believe a great big part of the creation he came to redeem is our work. After all, such work was a big part of the original grand plans and good purposes at the start of the story with Creation."

Ben's cell phone went off. "Excuse me just a minute." He stood up from the table, took a couple steps, paused, and then stepped outside the Dunkin' Donuts door. Maggie and Zach were so jazzed by these new discoveries, they continued buzzing on their potential implications for finding better meaning, joy, and service in their own daily jobs.

When Ben stepped back in the door and approached the table, his look showed concern, and his seasoned wrinkles were more pronounced. "Sorry, but 'have to put our caffeinated talk on hold for today. A patient over at the hospital is headed down for emergency surgery."

The threesome rose, gathered up Doc Ben's small library, tossed their cups, and headed out the doors. Ben paused before getting in his car, "I'm very intrigued and somewhat amused by the call. This is a woman whom I just met by chance, though I like to call these divine appointments." He tossed his deep-brown leather satchel onto the back seat. "She was a roommate to Barbara, a long-time patient I've been visiting off and on for several months. This roommate's name is Vicki, and she was only mildly receptive the couple times we chatted. But I guess she heard me praying with Barbara. So, she requested the nurses call me and ask me to now come pray with her. I never cease to be amazed at how God opens the doors of people's hearts."

They said quick goodbyes. Ben headed for the hospital. Zach and Mags jumped in his G37 and headed for Grandma's house. As they zoomed home, Zach could not resist continuing the deep conversation.

"*So*, star student, you received your wonderfully personalized affirmation for your love and work with all things furry." Maggie grinned a great big, goofy, bright-white smile. "Yes, I know. 'Hard to beat a direct link to Genesis 1 as total props for your life passion and vocation, eh? 'Knew that God wanted me to be a vet!'"

"I wanted to ask him about *me*, but we got cut short. Help me figure out how my architectural work has any eternal impact. What do you think, based on Doc Ben's explanations?"

"Well," Maggie offered, "I don't think he was trying to imply that everyone has to find absolute validation of their work through a match-up with a Bible passage. Instead, it seems there are biblical perspectives and principles that can help guide anything and everything people do by way of work."

"That makes sense," Zach agreed. "And I'm noticing a theme. Are you? It seems that no matter where someone is working, whether it's as a mechanic, like Marshall, or a hospital chaplain, like Doc Ben, they can and should make the people they work with a huge priority. It seems this is right at the heart of serving others, for advancing the kingdom, to the glory of God—a great big focus on cultivating strong relationships with people."

Maggie was nodding. "Yes, I find that concept very convicting and stretching, in light of how I've come to view my pets' owners. You heard my confession to Doc Ben. I'm pretty embarrassed, but it's true. I find most people who bring me their pets to be a real pain in the you-know-what. And I think I need to back up and reevaluate my attitude and approach with people. I see a lot of compassion and tenderness and openness flowing from your grandfather, Marshall, and Doc Ben."

Zach was nodding. Mags continued, "It seems like they genuinely love people and spend a significant amount of time and energy investing in people, alongside and outside of their regular work hours. And do you notice—across time, such relational investments seem to produce some pretty awesome results for Christ's kingdom?"

"Yes," Zach agreed. "I'm thinking I need to spend some more time praying for, caring for, and building better relationships with both coworkers and clients back at the firm. I've let myself become *so* consumed with the design grids and the buildings, and *not* so concerned about the people who help build them and eventually inhabit them. 'Sensing I need to start viewing my work as *my* mission field. I just really like creating the designs and then seeing the whole project executed. I wish *that* had some eternal meaning and lasting significance as well."

Maggie interjected with excitement. "Whoa! Wait a minute. If you think about it, I mean *really* think about it, this isn't an *either-or* issue, Zach. It seems it's a wonderful *both-and*." Zach wrinkled his face and gave Mags the *whatch-you-talkin-'bout* look.

"Yea, remember," Mags offered, "Ben said that Jesus came to redeem all creation, including the tangible work component, since that was part of original creation that was marred in the Fall. So, that would mean it's not just people's souls that can last forever. *What if* our actual physical work might also have lasting, eternal value?"

There was an excited, can't-believe-what-I'm-discovering tone in Mags' voice. "What if some of the buildings you build, as you build them to serve others, for his glory—and as Doc Ben was saying, for advancing his kingdom work in the world—*what if* in the final days, they might be redeemed along with all the rest of creation?"

"Hmm. That seems like a big proposition," Zach mused, "a pretty big stretch, Mags, especially when you remember that my preacher man uncle says it will all burn up at final judgment day."

Maggie furrowed her brow and laughed at the same time. "Yes, 'guess we're going to have to ask the good doctor his thoughts on this when we get together next time."

They pulled into Gram's drive. "I'm hungry!" Zach announced.

"You just inhaled *your* giant chocolate chip muffin and half of *mine*," Mags retorted. "How can you be hungry already?"

"It's lunchtime!" Zach replied.

Reflecting on Henry's Story, God's Story, and Your Story

1. Maggie was honest about her own love for animals *over* the pet owners. Do you view what you do at work as serving others out of authentic, Christ-like love? Identify two or three ways you can increase your genuine love and service for others.

2. Explore Genesis 2, with special focus on verse fifteen. Also read Isaiah 42:1–7, Matthew 12:15–21, and Philippians 2:1–11. How does this conceptual thread of being a worker/ servant, with a Christ-like outlook, challenge you and stretch you?

3. Wrestle with Doc Ben's explanation of *glory* and *glorify*. What are some practical, everyday implications for both your attitude toward God and your actions at work? How can your work help spotlight God, to make him more famous? Write down multiple ideas.

4. What are the connections between the *imago Dei* and the *missio Dei*? What does this mean for your daily work?

5. On the car ride home, Zach tells Mags he has noticed a theme running through the actions of Grandpa, Marshall, and Doc Ben: "a huge priority . . . a great big focus on cultivating strong relationships with people." Take further steps this week to cultivate stronger relationships with coworkers and other business contacts.

   What specifically do you plan to do? Schedule a breakfast, lunch, coffee, a walk on break-time, or golf next weekend.

   What next-level questions will you ask them in order to build rapport and get to know him/her better? Then take notes and commit to pray in light of your discoveries.

CHAPTER FIVE

Church at Work

They landed home in time to eat lunch with Grandma and several family members who were still sticking around. Some of the cousins and their kids had packed up and headed home in light of Grandpa's recent rally-back. Grandma placed a spread of fresh rolls, deli turkey and ham, provolone cheese, kettle chips, and pickle spears across the kitchen counter. As they all built sandwiches, Zach and Maggie excitedly reviewed their coffee time discoveries from the couple hours with Doc Ben.

After some time of just listening, Grandma spoke up. "It certainly seems you two are enjoying a heart-and-mind adventure, and one that's rather timely. Though he hasn't told me so, I think your grandfather must be mighty thrilled that you've met Ben and Marshall. He thinks the world of those guys, and I'm sure he's feeling very satisfied that you're discussing some deep things with them."

Zach laughed. "Yea, and the funny thing is how totally opposite these guys are. Marshall is your kind-of-crusty, country bumpkin, half-mechanic, half-trucker. Doc Ben, well obviously, he's the classic, well-educated, university-tenured, scholar-chaplain. And he's still busy in retirement, serving others in the medical field. It's obvious, though they're both very different, the deep biblical ideas and foundational practices create a common thread between them. So, they are both having big impact on what they both call their *mission fields*. And they both seem so confident in God's call on their lives to do exactly what they are doing, serving others, to God's glory, advancing Christ's kingdom. It's honestly very inspiring." Maggie nodded.

"It is indeed," Grandma said. "And believe it or not, Ben, Marshall, and your grandfather, well, they're not the only ones who have been thinking and doing life in such a unique way. It's all over our church now, so many people living this out at their jobs every day. Pastor Tom calls it a missional life."

"I've heard that term several times over the past couple years," Mags interjected. "I always thought of missions as being only a 'round the world, other-side-of-the-globe concept. Now, I'm starting to see that all of us, every person, no matter their profession, can plan his or her life to fulfill God's purpose, to be an agent of God's mission right there in their workplace and local community. In fact, I'm starting to think that in light of how many hours Christians spend in their workplaces, maybe this was God's plan all along."

Grandma chunked another piece of provolone and handed it to Zach. He loved cheese. Nodding in agreement with Maggie's thoughts, Grandma shared more. "Hardly a Sunday service goes by that we don't hear a new story of a workplace leader who is serving, caring, and sharing Christ with others at the office, or the mall, or whatever jobsite they're on. This missional focus has been involving people in every imaginable form of work. I'm serious. It's car mechanics, doctors, plumbers, stock traders, stay-at-home moms, corporate executives—anyone who really starts to *get it* that their job can be their mission field for the glory of God."

> *"I always thought of missions as being only a 'round the world, other-side-of-the-globe concept. Now, I'm starting to see that all of us, every person, no matter their profession, can plan his or her life to fulfill God's purpose, to be an agent of God's mission right there in their workplace and local community."*

"That's very cool," Zach interjected, "and certainly very different than how most churches seem to view people in their Monday through Friday jobs. I don't think most people in my church back in Valley Forge have any sense there's any connection between their work life and church life. And they certainly don't see any correlation with missions, aside from pastors wanting them to give money out of their paychecks in order to support global endeavors."

"It was the same way at our church," Gram said, "up until several years ago. And what's tremendous is when we see baptisms of those people who have been reached by Christ-followers at work. I will never forget the Sunday that Marshall got baptized. He was so nervous to tell his story, and he insisted on wearing his overalls into the water."

Maggie and Zach started laughing. "Oh, I'd love to have captured a picture of that," Mags exclaimed.

"I think we have one somewhere 'round here," Gram replied. "Marsh said no one had seen him in anything else in years. He stuttered a couple times while sharing his story, but he did a great job, just sharing from his heart. He cried. People cheered. And best of all, Grandpa was right there in the water and baptized him. Pastor Tom insisted. More than a few people have been miffed at Tom for letting lay folks baptize, but Tom says, 'If you bring 'em to Christ, you get to baptize 'em. That's all part of the Great Commission.' I had never thought of it that way before, but it makes sense. It's right there in Matthew 28:19–20, and those words are for all of us."

"That's *very* cool," Zach exclaimed. "I don't think I've ever seen anyone other than pastors baptize people."

"Yes, a lot of things have changed at our church in the past eight to ten years, primarily motivated by this whole missional thrust. Recently, Pastor Tom was in a whole big boiling tub of hot water because he's started *ordaining* ordinary people, everyday workers for their marketplace mission. At first, your grandpa and I were pretty put out as well. We thought, *Now that's crossing the line. Ordination is sacred, special for clergy. How dare he?* But then, we started to watch and listen deeper. Frankly, I was amazed at what I had missed across the years. Pastor Tom explained that according to the Bible, a big part of God's story is his blessing, creating a kingdom of priests. Tom preached a powerful message series from Genesis 12:1–3, Exodus 19:5–6, 1 Peter 2:9–21, and Revelation 5:9–10."

Zach interrupted. "Wow, that sounds like quite a big stretch of Scriptures to preach from. And honestly, Gram, I hate to admit it, but I can't tell you what any of those passages are about. How in the world do those have anything to do with ordination or missional living in the workplace? I get it that Jesus' Great Commission has big bearing, but hardly Genesis, Exodus, and especially Revelation. You've lost me."

Gram chuckled. "Don't feel bad, Grandson. I said the same thing when Tom announced those passages for the message series. And I can't possibly do justice to how he delivered the full explanation, but I can remember the basics. The gist is this: Jesus had a way of reading the Bible that was all about mission. In Luke 24:44–49, Jesus revealed that the Hebrew Scriptures, what we call Old Testament today, foretold not only Jesus' arrival as promised Messiah, but also his mission to all nations. Luke 24:46–47 proves very significant in understanding God's story of mission."

> *"Since the earliest pages of the Bible, God's story has included his purpose to form a beautiful mosaic of people into his kingdom."*

Zach grabbed his iPhone, tapped his Bible App and looked it up. "Verses forty-six and forty-seven say, 'This is what is written: The Messiah will suffer and rise from the dead on the third day, and repentance for the forgiveness of sins will be preached in his name to all nations, beginning at Jerusalem.'"

Suddenly, Zach went wide-eyed, and read it again silently. He gulped, and then read the final clause again, this time aloud and now with big emphasis. "*And repentance for the forgiveness of sins will be preached in his name to all nations.* That's *huge!*" Zach exclaimed.

"Yes, it's a huge concept. Well-said," Gram affirmed.

"I just never saw that before," Zach explained. "Jesus is saying . . . let me make sure I have this right . . . he's saying that the Old Testament was foretelling, pointing toward him *and his mission* to all nations!?"

Gram and Mags were grinning. Gram affirmed, "Yes, that's right. So that's where Old Testament passages like Genesis 12 and

Exodus 19, even some Psalms like Psalm 67 and others, become so important in the story. With Genesis 12, God commands Abram to go and be a blessing, and God promised Abram that all people groups, all nations would be blessed long-range through his family. Here's proof that people matter *so* much to God! In fact, Genesis 12 is so foundational to God's missional story that the Apostle Paul, in Galatians 3:6–9, calls it *the Gospel in advance.*"

"That's big as well!" Zach interrupted. "I always thought of the Gospel as just a *Jesus in the New Testament* concept. It never dawned on me that it was really the story God was unfolding throughout all of the Bible."

Gram nodded and continued. "Yes, the story of how that blessing for all people has unfolded becomes the big story of the whole Bible, with Christ Jesus and His redemptive mission as the central focus." She paused a moment, so the three of them could take a mental breath.

She continued. "Since the earliest pages of the Bible, God's story has included his purpose to form a beautiful mosaic of people into his kingdom."

Mags chimed in, "Doc Ben made a big deal this morning about the language of *ruling* in Genesis 1 and 2. Is this in any way related?"

"Probably so," Gram affirmed. "God has always intended for people to have a big leading influence, to make a real difference in the world. In Exodus 19:5–6, God labels people of the kingdom with a title. He calls them *priests*. And what do priests do? Priests bless. Priests serve and sacrifice. Priests serve others for the glory of God, to make God even more famous, truly magnified. Priests help connect people in dynamic ways with God's blessing."

"So what about the New Testament passages you mentioned?" Mags asked.

"Exceptional question." Gram was audibly excited by such an inquisitive thirst for knowledge shining through in a young woman. Since the time *she* was a young girl, Gram had loved to read. Now in her later years, she loved to encounter young women with such a kindred spirit for deep learning.

Gram continued. "Here's where the connection becomes extra exciting for us today. Like Paul connects the Gospel with the ancient Hebrew Scriptures in his letter to the Galatians, Peter connects this concept of priests in his teaching in 1 Peter 2:9–10. He insists that *all* Christ-followers, not just pastors and missionaries, are serving as a royal priesthood. And then from verses 11 and following, Peter proceeds to describe the various realms, including government leadership and masters and their servants. Current commentators believe we should apply that today to employers and employees."

Zach couldn't resist commenting. "I'd say there's some serious relevance for Christians at work."

"That's right," Gram agreed. "Peter says that everyday working Christians serve as priests, leading others to *see your good deeds and glorify God*. Ever since Pastor Tom's series, that phrase from verse 12 has stuck with me: *see your good deeds and glorify God.*"

"There it is again!" Zach exclaimed. "We were talking this morning with Doc Ben about this big idea of glorifying God through our work. Seems like it's all over the Bible."

"Yes," Gram replied. "Think on it! My good works, your everyday tasks and accomplishments—really everything we do each day—can help make God famous. Others can encounter his impressive character and actions, his shining presence. And they can personally experience more of him, making a real difference in their world. More people can come to deeply know Christ and begin to live for him in his kingdom, when I serve others like that. It's truly an exciting truth, an immense privilege, this role we get to play in the story, to bring him glory."

"So what about Revelation, Gram?" Zach tossed the question on the table. "I've always thought that book is primarily scary, gloomy . . . you know, the apocalyptic end of all things. How in the world does it have *anything* to do with missional living?"

Gram jumped to answer, and she had a spark of enthusiasm in her voice. "It's actually providing us with heavenly insights into the celebrations in heaven, celebrations over the mission accomplished, both already and yet to come. When we read it that way, it becomes very triumphant. Revelation 5:9–10 shows a climactic worship scene, proving that God's promises to Abraham back in

Genesis 12 are indeed now fulfilled. Can you pull that up on your iPhone, Zach?"

Zach tapped his App, searched, and read Revelation 5:9–10: "And they sang a new song, saying: 'You are worthy to take the scroll and to open its seals, because you were slain, and with your blood you purchased for God persons from every tribe and language and people and nation. You have made them to be a kingdom and priests to serve our God, and they will reign on the earth.'"

Zach paused, took a deep breath, and exclaimed, "Holy *crap!*" He quickly realized what he had just blurted in front of his grandmother. Across the years in their family, it was known that Gram would not tolerate the word *holy* vocalized to accompany anything other than God's name and worship. And she surely would not tolerate it matched up with a word like *crap.* Zach started to turn ten shades of red as he hung his head. "I'm *so* sorry, Gram." But to his amazement, as he looked up, she was laughing. So was Maggie. In fact, Mags had come off her chair, holding her stomach, as she laughed so hard. After a few more moments of laughter, Zach reached a hand to help her back in her chair at the kitchen table.

When everyday workers are ordained, these people are saying before God and the church, "We are committed to serving, praying for others, and sharing our faith in Christ with coworkers, clients, and our business contacts. And we are devoting ourselves to solid work ethics, and the kind of excellence at work that will pique curiosity because it really honors the Lord."

Grandma regrouped. "I think maybe in this case you can say that, Grandson, since there are a bunch of *holy, holy, holies* right before the verses we just read. I guess I'll allow it." The threesome laughed some more.

Zach explained, "I'm just honestly blown away by the correlation of all these concepts, coming to culmination right here. The redemption purchase through Christ's blood, people from every nation, a kingdom, priests who serve, and they will reign. Wow, it's all just so fully synthesized, the whole story fulfilled. I've never seen that!"

"I agree," Maggie seriously commented. "But what about ordination, Pastor Tom, and people being upset?"

"Oh yes," Gram answered. "That's where we started, didn't we. Well, ordination has been a long-held, centuries-old ceremony. You know, only performed to lay hands on and recognize those becoming official clergy. So the idea that you could pray over, commission, and set apart for God's service everyday folks like auto mechanics, truck drivers, doctors, garbage collectors, and corporate executives, well, that was well nigh unto heresy for a bunch of folks at our church."

Zach chimed in. "Yea, I can see why that would get some people's blood pressure boiling. What's happened?"

"Well, it's actually been fun to see," Gram explained. "Pastor Tom has just stuck to his guns and kept teaching this business of missional living, your workplace being your mission field, and he's kept on praying over and ordaining people who get serious about this. See, that's the amazing thing. In practice, it's just a special prayer of dedication, a commissioning, recognizing that these Jesus-followers know they are called and committed to living their faith on their jobs. When everyday workers are ordained, these people are saying before God and the church, 'We are committed to serving, praying for others, and sharing our faith in Christ with coworkers, clients, and our business contacts. And we are devoting ourselves to solid work ethics, and the kind of excellence at work that will pique curiosity because it really honors the Lord.' Throughout these several years, more and more people at church have started to realize, *what could be wrong with that?* They've started to see it's actually very biblical and Christ-honoring. How can anyone keep arguing with that?"

All of a sudden, there was a knock on the side door just off the kitchen.

"Who in the world?" Grandma whispered with a puzzled look. "I'm not expecting anyone."

She got up and opened the door. It was Uncle Clyde. Immediately, Zach rolled his eyes and his stomach began to churn with apprehension. Grandma invited him in. Zach said a polite hello, and Gram offered him a chair to join them at the kitchen table.

As he sat down, Zach could not help but notice that his patterned silk tie clashed with his suit pants and socks. His oversize body engulfed the antique chair. *I wonder if the chair will really hold up?* Zach thought to himself. He believed he could hear it squeaking more than normal, extra-stressing under the heavy load of his uncle's weight.

"Just stopping by to check on everyone and offer up some bold prayers of faith," Clyde explained as he settled in. The old chair screamed some more, and Zach cringed inside.

Gram courteously thanked him and proceeded to describe Grandpa's current positive condition.

"Well, praise the Almighty Lord who still heals!" Uncle Clyde continued with a verbose speech and recollection of some lines from an old song. "This world is not my home, I'm just a passin' through . . . the angels beckon me from heaven's open door, and I can't feel at home in this world any more."

It was obvious that such phrases were not all that comforting to Gram in this situation, though Uncle Clyde might have meant well. Once again, Zach thought, *He's so out of touch. What planet is he from? Obviously, not this one.* After a few moments of enduring the preacher talk, Zach had a flash of inspiration that held potential for their escape.

"Only one life, twill soon be past, only what's done for Christ will last." There was something of a reverberation in his vocal tone as he said it, as if he might have just entered the pulpit, at least in his own mind.

"Hey, Gram and Uncle Clyde, sorry, but Maggie and I need to scoot. I'm just remembering that Marshall said we should stop back down with the truck to work on those brakes. I'm not sure how many more days we can stay, and so we better go see him." Zach was hoping such an excuse was his ticket out of the conversation with Uncle Clyde, before he turned more personal with Zach. Zach quickly stood and so did Mags.

Uncle Clyde extended his gorilla-size hand toward Zach. "Remember, Son, and I'll keep saying it to you until it finally takes root in your heart. *Only one life, 'twill soon be past, only what's done for*

Christ will last." There was something of a reverberation in his vocal tone as he said it, as if he might have just entered the pulpit, at least in his own mind.

Zach did his best to feign a smile and nod. "Thanks, Uncle Clyde, for your thoughts and prayers for all of us." *That was very gracious of me*, Zach mused.

Out the door they went, quickly stepping into the gravel driveway and the shelter of Henry's cab.

"Oh, boy," Maggie exclaimed. "I see what you mean. Gives me the creeps. I'm sorry, he may mean well, but it's just so weird, what he says and how he says it."

"Yea, I don't want to talk about it," Zach replied, with fresh frustration in his voice. "Just need some air." He cranked down the window and turned the ignition key. It cranked but would not start. "What the . . . you aggravating hunk of junk!" He slammed his fist on the steering wheel.

Mags grinned. "Zach, remember, talk to him nice and tap the gas pedal."

Zach obeyed, but with toddler-like reluctance. He pounded the gas pedal very hard five times and spoke sarcastically, "Come on, Henry, you can do it. Start like a good old fella!" Sure enough, he came to life, and they headed for the open road.

Reflecting on Henry's Story, God's Story, and Your Story

1. Do you currently view and do your work as your primary mission field? If so, what makes this a reality? If not, what will it take for you to adopt that view and perform your work to serve others, to the glory of God?

2. Explore this string of Scriptures: Luke 24:44–49 (with focus on verse 47); Genesis 12:1–3; Exodus 19:5–6; 1 Peter 2:9–21; and Revelation 5:9–10.

Reflect on these questions:

What was unique about Jesus' way of reading the Old Testament?

What do you learn about Abram's blessing and the long-term impact?

What is the priestly connection between Exodus and 1 Peter?

How does Revelation 5:9-10 tie together the culmination of these missional concepts? Explain.

3. What does the overview of God's story you just saw teach you about missional living and your role in the story as it relates to your daily work? How are you motivated toward changes in your attitudes and actions at work?

4. Share your thoughts and opinions about the changes that took place through Pastor Tom's teaching and emphases across the years at Gram's church (e.g., ordinary workers living missional at their jobs, everyday folks baptizing people and being ordained for workplace mission, etc.). Do you personally find these changes bothersome or empowering?

5. Gram explained: "When everyday workers are ordained, these people are saying before God and the church, 'We are committed to serving, praying for others, and sharing our faith in Christ with coworkers, clients, and our business contacts. And we are devoting ourselves to solid work ethics, and the kind of excellence at work that will pique curiosity because it really honors the Lord.'"

How important are these commitments to you? What difference does it make when a Christian delivers an exceptional product and service, to the glory of God? What difference would it make for you to currently make such commitments?

CHAPTER SIX

Fixin' Brakes & Fixin' Culture

Within a few minutes of their arrival, Marshall had pulled the F-100 into his garage. Very quickly, he had Henry's rear axle up on jack stands, and he was tearing into the brake assembly. Rusty, crusty brake pads and broken calipers were yanked off, making way for the new, much safer stopping equipment.

Marshall packed some fresh Mixture No. 79 into his pipe and lit up. "By golly, if I didn't love Fords so much, I'd sell my farm and garage and join you, Miss Maggie, caring for critters back there in Pennsylvania. I've sure loved my mutts 'cross the years, and look 'round ya. Sure do love this bunch of cats." One was already walking across Henry's tailgate like he was doing a high-wire act at the circus. "But I do love Fords. And Ford vehicles and those Ford owners, plus a few truck driver friends—well, they're my mission field, ya know."

Zach and Mags noticed Marshall repeating himself from time to time, some early signs of age setting in. But each time, he shared his same mission focus with the same enthusiasm, as if he had never told them about it before. They couldn't help but chuckle inside at such a multi-sensory blend of sweet-smelling tobacco, grease, gasoline, and talk of God's mission.

"You kids are welcome to go if you're bored," Marshall offered. "Brake jobs can be pretty dull, but you're also welcome to stay a spell. Just takes me a little while per wheel, 'specially on old Ford brakes like these."

"We're very good to hang out, watch and talk, if that's ok." Zach saw the garage and brake job as a welcome refuge from the Uncle Clyde invasion up the road at Gram's. Plus, Zach was still curious about a couple things, and he decided to dive in with deeper questions for Marshall.

"So, Grandma and Grandpa told us more about your baptism and your life changes, and how you've

> *"I do love Fords. And Ford vehicles and those Ford owners, plus a few truck driver friends. Well, they're my mission field, ya know."*

been a big blessing to other mechanics and truckers. I'm wondering, Marsh, what's most grabbed you at church? Gram explained to us over lunch today about Pastor Tom's unique teaching and his ordaining regular workers. I'm just curious, what grabs guys like you? What gets you excited about your mission field, as you call it? Do you mind me asking? Can you talk as you work?"

Marshall's belly shook as he replied, "You bet I can talk. I've learned to talk and turn wrenches at the same time. It's a gift." Now all three chuckled.

"For me, it's Jesus most, his life an' teachin'. Pastor Tom shares all his stuff 'bout mission from the Old Testament, and that's mighty fine and all. But for me, I'm so stirred in my heart by Jesus' teachin' on the kingdom. Of course, it's ex'ra good when you re-alize Jesus himself worked in a shop, probably wood-workin' and maybe sculpture craftin', before he ever preached a sermon. He was busy learnin' from his dad, Joseph, and then he apparently ran the carpentry business for a bunch of years before he started teachin' disciples, workin' miracles, and all."

Mags couldn't contain her sudden amazement. "Here we go again. I'm honestly stunned by these discoveries. I guess they've been there in the Bible all along, but they just haven't registered in my mind. So, Jesus knew business and the workplace, didn't he, based on his own upbringing?"

"Yup," Marshall continued. "And he knew people, business people of all stripes and smells. He knew job backgrounds for farmin' folk, politic types, land exec's, tax agents, fishermen, and many more. That's why when he's teachin' an' preachin' in the Gospels, so many of his stories 'bout the kingdom have to do with workin' folks. And they're not just nice stories with double meaning. He really is talkin' bout how his foll'ers work and handle money and care for other people, so more people can come into his kingdom." Marshall paused, took a long draw on his pipe and blew a fresh ring of sweet smoke in the air.

He continued. "And all over the Gospels, when he's talkin' 'bout his kingdom, he's also spendin' time with folks, eatin' meals with 'em, drinkin' with 'em, just relatin' to 'em with both grace and truth. That seems to be Jesus' plan, how he works for more people to come in. Dat's really mighty marv'lous, if you ask me!" Marsh was sharing deep from his heart. "For me, over my early years, I learned Fords from master mechanics. And then I taught Fords to other young mechanics, and by golly, it grabs my soul that Jesus' master thought was the kingdom, and his mission was makin' it bigger with more people blessed to come on in. He was busy changin' lives, changin' hearts, and really, changin' culture."

He chuckled again, and this time it was an extra-hearty laugh. Obviously for some reason, he was amused by his own comment. Mags and Zach looked confused.

"I know, my *culture* comment prob'ly sounds funny comin' from a greasy ol' feller like me, but it's true. Jesus' kingdom focus can help change people's whole world, includin' makin' the culture better. That's what he was busy teachin' his learners in his Sermon on the Mount, a whole bunch of ways that they'd be a changin' on the inside and then helpin' that change spread to others. He was sayin', *If you're in my kingdom, you'll be world changers, makin' a real dif'rence.* I love Matthew 5, verses 14 through 16, 'You are the light of the world . . . let your light shine before others, that they may see your good deeds and glorify your Father in heaven.' Matches right up with what ol' Paul says to those Corinthians, 'do it all for the glory of God.' And if ya think on it, it's a glory thing, really, that even guys like me can learn the kingdom from Jesus, the Master.

As my life's changin' and my good work is *really* good and serves others, they end up seeing how famous God really is. They're seein' his glory."

He paused and puffed again. Zach and Mags were sitting on two dusty old folding chairs and sipping ice cold Cokes from vintage glass bottles. Marsh had dispensed them from an original soda pop machine that had to have been in the corner of Marshall's shop since the 1960s. The machine still just took one quarter per Coke, though Marshall bypassed that by just opening the door and pulling them from the slot. These days, it was really a glorified cooler. Suddenly, Zach realized that Marshall was already on the fourth wheel's brake set. Indeed, he could work and talk at the same time, and he could still work at a rapid pace. *Amazing energy and skill,* Zach thought.

> *He paused and puffed again. Zach and Mags' were sitting on two dusty old folding chairs and sipping ice cold Cokes from vintage glass bottles. Marsh had dispensed them from an original soda pop machine that had to have been in the corner of Marshall's shop since the 1960s.*

"What's thrillin' to me," Marshall continued, "is that this whole mission thing isn't just for guys like me 'round these Ohio parts. Did you know that a bunch of construction fellers from church, young'ns in their twenties and thirties, have started backin' a new construction company that's open'n in Haiti. Ever since that hor'ble quake back when, people been buildin' quick houses down there, more like lean-tos and such. But in the past couple years, they been sayin' at church that the whole country's changin'. More people from the USA been pourin' lots of relief and Jesus' kinda hands-on love there, and also teachin' people 'bout Jesus. Now, the whole culture is gettin' more solid, and there's people actually fixin' to build nicer homes. So these guys got the idea of actually startin' a build comp'ny in Haiti. They plan to hire local workers, build new friends as they build those homes, and help other people come in the kingdom. 'Long the way, those boys actually talkin' bout helpin' build new churches there too."

"That is *very cool* to hear." Zach responded with sincere excitement in his voice. "I don't think I'd have ever dreamed of such a hands-on company having a missional impact, but that makes real sense."

"Yup, it does," Marshall continued. "I've done breakfast with a couple of those young fellers, and they'll 'ventually be makin' real money, after a few years. They should be gettin' their original dollars back, plus makin' some new money. 'Least that's their plans. But the money won't be just for them. They say they're insisting lots of that new money'll be helpin' the local workers, their families, and helpin' the whole 'conomy in Haiti grow stronger. Sounds like a mighty good plan, servin' others for God's glory."

> "So these guys got the idea of actually startin' a build comp'ny in Haiti. They plan to hire local workers, build new friends as they build those homes, and help other people come in the kingdom. 'Long the way, those boys actually talkin' 'bout helpin' build new churches there too."

Marshall hooked a final spring, tightened a bolt, and wiped a clean rag across the shiny new brake pad. "Ok, time to bleed these brakes and you'll be good to go. Have you ever helped bleed brakes, Zach?"

Mags started laughing. She gave a quick-witted reply. "Careful, Marshall. Remember, he's a dangerous man with tools in hand."

"Excuse me!" retorted Zach. "I'll have you know that this is something I *do* know how to do. I did it with Grandpa many times!"

Marshall started chuckling again, his belly shaking like a bowl full of jelly. "What he's not tellin' you, Miss Maggie, is that he doesn't have to lift a single tool. Just sit in the cab and push the brake pedal, an' hold it as I tell him *up* or *down* on the pedal."

"Oh, I see. He conveniently left that part out," Mags replied as she gave Zach a shove on the shoulder. He shoved back, and it landed as more of a hug between them.

"Jump in the truck cab, Zach," Marshall said. "And now lis'n to what I yell. We're bleedin' air out of these here new brake lines." Within twenty minutes, they had finished the job.

"That should do it. I reckon he's all safe for you kids, so you can stop quieter now, and quit hittin' folks' fences." Marshall laughed at his own tease. "Tell me again, what do you call this old guy? Herman?"

"No." Mags corrected with a grin. "I named him Henry, after Henry Ford. Not real original, I know, but 'seemed to fit.'"

"Well, I 'gree," Marshall replied warmly. "Seems to fit. I like him. Sad to think you'll get such shabby gas mileage when you drive him back to PA. But back when Ford Motors built these F-100s in the 1970s, gasoline was still under a buck, prob'ly closer to fifty cents a gallon in 1977. Why, I remember when it was 'bout a nickel, back in the day."

"That's unbelievable," Zach exclaimed. "Can you imagine if we could time travel with a whole bunch of gas cans?"

Marshall smiled and mused for a moment. "I actually think the real Henry Ford would be pretty 'mazed at what's goin' on today with 'lectric cars and other new-fangled forms of fuel. Hardly anyone talks 'bout it, but Ford was really ahead of his time. Before he died, he was workin' on tryin' to make other fuels. He thought cars and trucks ought to have options to burn things other than gasoline. Not too many other folks saw it necessary, since oil seemed 'bundant and so cheap.

"That's fascinating!" Zach was shaking his head with an incredulous look. "Say, Marshall. I apologize to have to run, but I just realized, it's already after six. Gram said we would scoot to see Gran'pa after dinner.

Marshall was very tender and passionate now. "Just do some figurin' on who you can bless. I've learned that takes some plannin'. Doesn't jus' happen. Plan for it. Eat with 'em. Care for 'em, pray for 'em, and share Jesus with 'em, with both your hands and your words."

She's probably wondering what happened to us. This has been great. Thanks so much. Now what do we owe you for the brake job as well as the work from the other day?"

Marshall grinned as he tapped out cold tobacco in his hand and wiped his pipe clean. "Nothin'. And don't start arguin' with me now." Marshall put his hand up. He could sense Zach about to protest. "I already had the spare set of rotors and pads on the shelf over there. 'Member, I'm the Ford guy, and I just love doin' this to bless folks, includin' you. I'm so thankful for your granddad's impact in my life. God's been so good to me. Times like this are jus' my way of sayin' thanks to the good Lord and bringin' him glory. Just make sure now in your hearts you're impressed with Jesus, and promise me you'll go bless somebody else."

Zach and Mags were nodding their heads. "We will. Most definitely," Zach promised. "But . . ." Zach was still trying to argue, but Marshall verbally rolled right over him.

"Make *him* famous. Help others come to Jesus, come into his kingdom." Marshall was very tender and passionate now. "Just do some figurin' on who you can bless. I've learned that takes some plannin'. Doesn't jus' happen. Plan for it. Eat with 'em. Care for 'em, pray for 'em, and share Jesus with 'em, with both your hands and your words."

Now, all Mags and Zach could do was smile. "I don't think you better even try to argue with him about paying," Maggie coached.

"I know. No use. Lost cause." Zach shook his head and laughed with great respect and awe at such generosity. Marshall grinned.

"Wait!" Marshall shouted as Zach gave Henry the five foot pumps and turned his key. The motor was purring now. "There is one thing you can do for me, and I'm very serious. Go down to the ODMV tomorrow and get your temporary tags, registration and all, and then make sure you bring him back to me one more time before you head back to PA."

"Oh, don't worry," Zach responded. "I don't think we'll be driving him back to PA this time. I have my G37, and I think Henry is best-suited for staying in the Buckeye state right now."

"Well, that's just it," Marshall explained. "There are at least five, heck, maybe ten other things I really ought to check out on him to make him truly ready for over-the-road, 'specially for a long run. Promise to bring him back."

Zach and Mags could tell that Marshall truly got attached to the vehicles he worked on, especially the ones like Henry. "We promise," Zach replied. And he sensed there was more motivation than simply needing some more Ford work to accomplish. He obviously enjoyed their company and conversation. And Zach knew it was mutual.

Reflecting on Henry's Story, God's Story, and Your Story

1. Marshall shares with Mags and Zach how he is most moved by Jesus' example and teaching. Survey these examples of Jesus' kingdom behavior and lessons: Matthew, chapters 5–7; Matthew 9:9–13; and Luke 19:1–27.

   What do you learn about Jesus' perspective on his kingdom and mission?

   What do you see in Jesus' example of relational cultivation with people?

   What do you discover regarding work/service in Christ's kingdom?

2. Develop three to five personal commitments for your own work/service in Christ's kingdom. State them as action-oriented goals.

3. What do you think about Marshall's concept, his idea that a big part of Christ's kingdom agenda is "changin' culture?" Do you agree or disagree? Why?

4. Reflect on the example of the young businessmen starting a construction company in Haiti. Have you ever considered involvement in a global business initiative that holds kingdom purposes for the glory of God? Why or why not? What would it take for you to get involved in such a kingdom endeavor?

5. When they've finished Henry's brake work, Marshall wraps up their conversation with this challenge: "Just do some figurin' on who you can bless. I've learned that takes some plannin'. Doesn't jus' happen. Plan for it. Eat with 'em. Care for 'em, pray for 'em, and share Jesus with 'em, with both your hands and your words."

    How does his challenge to Zach and Mags challenge you? What are your intentional plans to further cultivate relationships and glorify God this week?

CHAPTER SEVEN

The Story Buried in the Attic

The visit with Grandpa after dinner was a bit overwhelming. They had a few moments of good conversation with him, but it was obvious that his strength was waning. The doctor came in for night rounds and had a serious conversation with Gram out in the hall. When they were ready to leave, they found themselves extra-grateful for the bonus time and the enlivened, lengthy conversations of previous days. There would not likely be many more of that depth or length. The doctor's explanations were tough to swallow.

As they drove home, Gram was quiet, and once or twice she appeared to wipe back tears, trying to remain composed. Zach was reflecting deep inside and seemed to be gulping back some of his own tears. At one point, Mags reached over and grabbed his hand. He squeezed hers back and held tight. She did not let go.

When they arrived home, Gram said, "How about some hot tea? 'Too late for coffee, but I sure could use a good cup of tea." She started the teakettle on the back burner. Before long, it was whistling, and she was pouring everyone a steaming hot cup. It was obvious that Gram was ready to talk about something other than Grandpa's declining health and the hospital regimen.

"So how did your work go over at Marshall's? You didn't tell me. How's the old pickup coming along?"

Zach shared the highlights of working brakes, but he skipped the other boorish mechanical details. He stressed his gratitude, but then added, "You know, Gram, it's always so much more when you're there at Marshall's. He told us his own take on what's happening at your church with Pastor Tom's whole missional thrust. Marshall shared what grabs him personally through Jesus' kingdom teaching and how Jesus spent time with people. And he also told us the incredible business start-up those guys from your church are doing in Haiti. That's amazing. I think I want to follow that and see if maybe I could somehow help out in some way."

Gram smiled and responded, "That would be great. 'Bet that would be right up your alley, Grandson—a real match with God's call on your life and how he wired you with passion for architecture, blending people and buildings. That could be very exciting. I can introduce you to one of those guys, and they can give you more information."

Mags looked at Zach with a silly grin and shrugged her shoulders. "Sounds like this involves Scooby Doo and the Mystery Machine," she playfully quipped.

"I'd like that, Gram. Thanks." Zach's face lit up with obvious enthusiasm at the prospects. "And of course, with Marshall, I'm learning there's always some fun, bonus information you discover."

"Oh, of course," Grandma agreed with a laugh and a nod. "He's always full of historical footnotes and anecdotes."

"Yea," Zach continued. "He told us about how Henry Ford was ahead of his time, researching and suggesting alternative fuel sources. That's all over the news these days, but apparently Ford was working on it way back then."

"Indeed, he was." Gram paused and gave a whimsical look. "That reminds me of something." Her smile broadened and her face morphed into a playfully mysterious expression, like she was hatching a scheme. She reached for the cabinet door next to the kitchen table and removed two flashlights.

"There's something you kids might find interesting related to all of this," Gram suggested. "You'll have to do a little hunting, some detective work of sorts. Are you up for it?"

Mags looked at Zach with a silly grin and shrugged her shoulders. "Sounds like this involves Scooby Doo and the Mystery Machine," she playfully quipped.

"Not really," Gram responded with a laugh. "But it does mean a trip up the stairs to the attic."

Zach bolted to his feet. "I haven't been up there in years. I'm game! What are we looking for?"

Gram was delighted that he was eager for the hunt. "Up there somewhere is a very old, rough-hewn, rather large, wooden box. I seem to recall some lettering, though the paint is probably faded by now. But it should still be readable. I think the painted label includes an old family name, *Gabbey,* the state letters *NY* from a time it was shipped to New York State. And I believe maybe even the letters *Congo* are painted on it. That's where it was was built."

Zach gave Gram an extremely curious look. "That's it? We're looking for a crate from Africa?" He was puzzled.

"Not really a crate," Grandma clarified. "It's more of a trunk, though very plain. If my memory serves me correctly, the handles are simply a rough, worn rope, and it has a heavy, hinged lid."

"And that's what we're looking for?" Zach asked. "Find it and haul it down? How heavy is this thing?"

"No, no," Gram corrected. "Find it and find what's inside! Many things have been removed over the years, and now, there are just a few remaining items. You are looking for a yellowed envelope with a letter inside. If you find it, don't open the envelope. Just bring it back down with the letter inside."

Zach led the way. Mags was stepping behind him, slowly ascending the attic stairs. Halfway up, her flashlight went black. Dead batteries. She grabbed Zach's hand.

Just then, Zach's flashlight went out. "What in the world . . . Oh no!" Zach exclaimed.

Mags let out a short screech, and she pulled closer to him.

Zach switched his light back on, and Maggie could see his ornery grin around the dusty edges of the flashlight glow. She pounded his arm with her fist, exclaiming, "You are *so* rotten, Zachary David! *Why* do I hang out with you?" But then, to his surprise, she locked her fingers with his and pulled even closer to his side. Though she could not see it, now he was grinning inside with great glee.

They brushed aside cobwebs near the top of the stairs and then shined the light out across the attic. Rustic wood beams spanned the top of the old house. The floor was strewn with a variety of family antiques, a stack of hatboxes, and an old coat tree. *Where in the world can that trunk be?* Zach wondered.

They scanned the edges, back under the eaves. Nothing. They stood still, and suddenly, out of nowhere, they heard something scurry and squeak. Tiny feet. "It's a mouse," Zach reassured. "Nice, how comforting," Mags sarcastically quipped. "Did you bring a trap with cheese? Wouldn't matter. You'd have already eaten the cheese. Perhaps we should have borrowed one of Marshall's cats?" Mags was obviously not scared, not in the least.

"Come on, don't you want to just take a peak?" Maggie coaxed. And she flashed a quick, convincing smile. "She had to know we'd look." "Ok, but quick," Zach caved, "and never let her know we looked."

Just then, they came upon a massive pile of Christmas decor, which seemed to be covering something. Zach shoved aside several cardboard boxes, each labeled in Gram's distinctive cursive: *tinsel & garland, X-mas angels,* and one that simply read *wrap & scrap.* He shined the light closer to the object. Sure enough, he could make out black, muted lettering. There was no mistaking the label. Amid other faded letters, it still clearly read *Gabbey.*

Mags carefully lifted a pile of ornament boxes from atop the trunk, set them aside, and looked into Zach's eyes. "Well, go ahead. Open it," she encouraged. Zach lifted the lock latch with ease, and then grabbed the heavy lid.

"'Must be what Indiana Jones feels like before he enters a cave. Here goes," he announced with an air of courageous anticipation.

Zach slowly lifted the lid. A warmish, closed-much-too-long, stale smell emanated from the wooden vault, along with a rogue burst of dust. "Can you hold it open, please?" Zach choked through the dust. "That way I can look."

"Of course," Mags snapped back playfully. "Geesh, you're *so* needy. Go ahead. Do all the fun parts of the adventure. Allow me to hold the lid for you. 'Wouldn't want it to fall on your precious head.'" Her gift of sarcasm was shining brighter than ever.

Zach poked the flashlight deeper and stuck his head inside. Almost climbing in, he pushed aside a string bundle of old LIFE magazines, a dried-up box of *Arm and Hammer Baking Soda*, and several handmaid doilies. There it was. A stained, weathered envelope, extremely old, and very yellow. Zach snatched it from the deepest corner of the box, glanced 'round quickly, and pulled his head out of the pine cave. He took the lid from Mags' hands.

"Thanks much," he politely said, and closed it tight.

Maggie fumed, "I could have done that, Sherlock!"

"I'm sorry. My latent control issues, coming out again." Zach feigned an apology. "You're such a good sport, Watson. Now, let's go, and quick."

"Wait a minute," Maggie shot back. "Aren't we going to read the letter?"

"Not up here. Not without Gram. You heard her, didn't you?" Zach was always a rule-keeper at heart.

"Come on, don't you want to just take a peak?" Maggie coaxed. And she flashed a quick, convincing smile. "She had to *know* we'd look."

"OK, but quick," Zach caved, "and never let her know we looked."

They pulled back the tucked flap and wisped out the letter. A tri-folded sheet emerged, just as yellowed and crisp as the dusty, dry envelope. They stared at the page. The writing was scrolled, old flair, indiscernible. They could make out nothing but a few words in the archaic cursive on the page. Though the embossed letterhead itself might be legible, the darkness rendered it pointless to try to make out its meaning.

"See, Gram was right," Zach said with a smug told-you-so. "We need her help to decipher anything about this."

Slowly, step-at-a-time, they descended the attic stairs, making sure to not stumble and tumble. Deep down, they both knew they were slowly savoring each step, holding each other's hands ever so tightly.

Little did they know the letter they were about to read would create an even deeper, newfound bond of love for the story and mission of God—a remarkable connection between a famous piece of history, Zach's own family legacy, and his possible future in that amazing story.

Reflecting on Henry's Story, God's Story, and Your Story

1. Survey some more of Jesus' kingdom behavior and lessons: Matthew 25:14–30; Matthew 28:16–20; and Luke 15.

   What do you learn about Jesus' perspective on his kingdom and mission?

   What do you see in Jesus' example of relational cultivation with people?

   What do you discover regarding work/service in Christ's kingdom?

2. In light of these new discoveries, prayerfully revisit and revise the three to five personal commitments (begun last chapter) for your own work/service in Christ's kingdom. State them as action-oriented goals.

3. Ask God to help you see more of where he is already at work in your daily business, and how he can use you there as an even greater missional influence for his glory.

4. Courageously take a next step in relational cultivation with one or two coworkers, clients, or other work contacts this week. Don't rush or "cram" Jesus at your friend, but watch for opportunities to either . . .

   Offer to pray for her/him on a special need, *or*

   Offer to help her/him in a tangible way, at work or off-the-job, *or*

   As you sense it's appropriate, share pieces of your own faith story, relating how Jesus has changed your life.

5. Have fun speculating. From whom and to whom do you think the letter is written? What do you think the letter might say?

CHAPTER EIGHT

Hard Work & Significant Impact

"Got it!" Zach exclaimed upon reaching the bottom of the stairs. He and Mags stepped into the kitchen. "Gram! We found the letter!" Zach announced with a tone of triumph. But Gram was nowhere to be found.

They headed into the living room and called for her. Nothing. Zach walked back to the kitchen and noticed his phone lying on the table. Apparently, in his excitement, he had left it there before heading to the attic. He had one new call.

He touched *Phone* and *Voicemail.* "Hello, Zach. It's Gram. The hospital called and said I should come. 'Realize I left you kids in the attic, but I just grabbed my keys and ran." Zach could sense a serious shaking in her voice, on the edge of tears. "You two can come if you want. The nurse said that Grandpa seems less responsive. 'Love you. Come on over or call me."

They grabbed keys and jumped in the G37. Fortunately, the hospital was only a twelve-minute drive. It seemed like they made it in five. When Maggie reminded Zach he was speeding, he muttered something about *just using all the horses available.*

And they got there just in time. In future hours and days, they would reflect on the timing with great gratitude. When they entered the hospital room, Gram was seated and pulled up very close to Grandpa. They could tell that she was saying goodbye. Zach and Maggie held back, but Gram motioned for them to come closer. Stepping to the foot of his bed, they all began to cry.

"Go ahead," Gram whispered to him. "Go be with Jesus. He's right there waiting for you. Then go see your mom, and Grandma and Grandpa." She was speaking through a steady stream of tears now. Grandpa was listening. "Then go horseback riding with a bunch of your buddies. They'll be eager to ride."

Grandpa had grown up training and riding horses, and he had loved to gallop through open fields. He had often talked about how thrilled he was to know there would be horses in heaven. In the next moment, he took a deep breath. It was obvious that with that one, he galloped home.

Zach and Maggie stepped toward Gram, and they all hugged, and wept, and held each other tight.

The next days were filled to the brim with the details, conversations, and raw emotions of preparing for the funeral. All the aunts, uncles and cousins returned. The service proved to be a fitting memorial. Afterward, many people commented that it was certainly a genuine celebration of all Jesus had accomplished in and through Grandpa's life. Amidst heartfelt tears, there were plenty of great stories and laughter.

"Phil certainly loved good hard work. God's grace worked through him. And he indeed lived his life to the glory of God, eager to know that what he accomplished would last into eternity."

Doc Ben officiated the service, and just as everyone anticipated, he shared moving words recounting God's grace: "This grace worked so effectively, not only saving Phil's soul, but allowing him to live a life of great meaning and real significance. He served others for the glory of God. Phil was able to say along with the Apostle Paul in 1 Corinthians 15:10, 'But by the grace of God I am what I am, and his grace to me was not without effect. No, I worked harder than all of them—yet not I, but the grace of God that was with me.'"

By now, there was hardly a dry eye in the room. People were nodding their heads in agreement. Ben continued, "Phil certainly loved good hard work. God's grace worked through him. And he indeed lived his life to the glory of God, eager to know that what he accomplished would last into eternity."

At the graveside, once the final amen was said, Zach made sure to thank Doc Ben. "You're very welcome. We're all going to miss him, and it's so good to know we'll see him again when we join him in heaven." Ben's words were sincere through and through. With reassurance, he said, "You know, that's our solid hope because of our faith in Christ." Zach nodded with knowing agreement and his own personal confidence.

"And I seem to recall that we have an unfinished cup of conversation, don't we?" Ben asked.

Maggie had just joined them. "We most certainly do," she chimed in, "And we both have fresh questions, *big* questions. Hope you're ready." She flashed a mischievous grin.

"That's great," Ben replied with a smile. "Bring it on! In case you haven't noticed, I enjoy great questions and robust dialogue. When are you two headed back to Pennsylvania?"

"'Probably will stick around another four or five days, so we can certainly get together," Zach answered. "Let's plan on it!"

Reflecting on Henry's Story, God's Story, and Your Story

1. At Grandpa's funeral, Doc Ben shares from 1 Corinthians 15:10. Look it up and explore the context, all of 1 Corinthians 15. What ideas stand out to you?

How does the following idea stir you, challenge you, or motivate you?

I can work hard and be effective, with God working through me by his grace!

How does the idea of Christ's resurrected body and your own resurrection someday supply you with renewed hope in the glory to come?

Why do you think Paul concludes this chapter with a call to faithful, steadfast, stellar work (1 Corinthians 15:58)?

2. Based on your discoveries from above, list several personal implications for living an even more integrated life. What needs to shift in your own attitude and actions?

3. Evaluate your current cultivation with coworkers and other business contacts. Review your notes.

   What are you learning about your friends?

How are you praying for them?

Is anyone's curiosity piqued yet?

Are they asking you any questions yet related to faith?

What will you do next to further build trust and have missional influence for Christ's glory?

What will it take for you right now in your daily work to "let nothing move you" and "always give yourself fully to the work of the Lord?" (1 Corinthians 15:58)

CHAPTER NINE

Henry & George

B ack at Gram's that evening, family members continued to
reminisce with an accompanying mix of hearty laughs and
heartfelt tears. Uncle Clyde was there, but he was strangely quiet.
His large presence was known, but he was certainly not obnoxious
or acting in his normal, bowl-you-over, preacher man ways. Gram
had simply requested that he say grace at the all-family meal in
the church fellowship hall, but no other speaking roles were re-
quired of him. *My grandmother is indeed very wise,* Zach thought
to himself.

As Uncle Clyde left, Zach actually found himself mildly impressed at his uncle's level of restraint. Not once had he leveraged
the event as an opportunity to rehearse his infamous "only one life"
quote. As the door closed at Clyde's exit, Zach exhaled with a deep
sigh of relief. *Yesss! 'Made it through, without experiencing the hu-
miliation of the quotation.*

Only Zach's parents, plus another aunt and uncle decided to
stay that night at Gram's. All of Zach's grown cousins decided to
either head home or find other spots to stay the night. The house
began to quiet down around ten o'clock. Predictably, Gram announced she was brewing some hot tea and asked if anyone wanted
some.

"Count us in," Zach replied. He and Mags settled in at the kitchen table. All other boarders had retired for the night, exhausted and ready for some shut-eye.

Gram poured hot water, and the tea bags began to steep. "It was a beautiful day, kids," Gram reflected. Her eyes were still red. "A hard day, yes, but a good one. Your grandpa would be happy. I mean he *must* be. We all spoke words that deeply honor Jesus, and we sang his favorite hymns. And deep down, *I'm* thrilled we're remembering your grandpa's life in these ways."

Zach jumped in. "Absolutely right, Gram. So many people came out for the service, and *so* many people shared their reflections of knowing and loving him. And did you notice? It seems that dozens were impacted throughout the years. So many reflected how they knew Grandpa from his various business endeavors. Several of those guys shared that they follow Christ today because of Grandpa and Marshall eating breakfast with them over at the truck stop. It's very moving—all those people and their stories. Truly, Grandpa did amazing work for Christ's kingdom. He really did."

Grandma was smiling. Then the look on her face shifted, as if she was ready for a new conversation.

"Say, I seem to recall us sitting right here about five days ago, and you two were headed to the attic on an adventure. I have to say, you've shown the utmost restraint and sensitivity to not bring it up." They both laughed. Gram continued, "But I'm OK now. 'Could actually use a change of topic before bed. So did you find it?"

Zach lit up with enthusiasm. "We think we did. Let me go grab it." He disappeared for a moment and returned with the yellow envelope and handed it over to Gram.

"So what do you think of it," she asked. Mags and Zach stared at each other and their eyes widened. *What do we say?*

Gram grinned. "I don't suppose you didn't look, *did* you?"

Zach hung his head. Mags giggled. "How did you know we'd look?" Mags asked through her sort-of-embarrassed grin.

"Easy," Gram quickly answered, "I told you *not* to look, but you were alone in the attic, so you were bound to look. And on top of that, you've now had five days to battle the temptation. Who wouldn't sneak a peak?"

"'Doesn't matter,'" Zach shrugged. "The handwriting is wicked cursive, like something from the Dark Ages."

"So we couldn't make it out anyway," Maggie added. "Don't worry. We received no satisfaction in opening it, and we've got *no* clue what it has to do with Henry Ford. But thanks for the creepy mystery trip up there. Really, we enjoyed the quest."

"I'm *sure* you did," Grandma answered with a mischievous smirk. She had not missed their increasing flirtation with one another since they'd arrived. Though they were grown-up young adults, they were flirting like they were thirteen-year-olds. The romantic tension was unmistakable.

"OK, so what are we looking at here?" Zach quickly changed the subject.

"Well, let's start with the letterhead. Take a look. Does that ring any bells?" Gram questioned.

Zach and Mags both read aloud: "Tuskegee Institute, Alabama, Founded by Booker T. Washington." They paused to think.

Zach offered tentatively, "I seem to recall from U.S. History class, Washington founded the school for blacks, or as it says on the letterhead, 'for colored young men and women.' And of course, that was revolutionary for the times."

"That's right," Gram affirmed. "So this is letterhead from that school. Now let me read you the rest of it aloud. Believe it or not, early in the twentieth century, everyone's handwriting looked much like this—very scrolled and artistic. No one texted or tweeted. You wrote letters whenever you wanted to communicate, long distance or short distance. You took great pride in your penmanship. It was part of what made your personal character unique."

"I get that," Zach responded. "Even today, there's still some serious recognition and respect for the higher artistic flair present in certain designers' preliminary sketch style, along with their lettering to label plans, plus their signatures in the corners. Pretty cool. I've worked to develop my own *John Hancock* flair."

Gram smiled and nodded. "So, here it is. I'll read it for you." She began to read, slowly and thoughtfully. "It is dated *August 13, 1931.*"

My Dear Mr. Johnston, . . . She paused for comment.

"Do you know who the letter is written to? 'Recognize the name?'"

Mags looked clueless and shook her head *no*.

But Zach jumped in enthusiastically: "Sure I do, that's *your* grandfather, my *great great* grandfather. Dad and Mom have shown me pictures of them, and years ago, when I was very little, I recall Great Grandma Janet telling stories about her parents."

Zach tried again, and suddenly, his eyes widened. Not only could he read the signature, but suddenly, crucial pieces of high school history were flooding back.

"That's right, very good," Gram responded. "And across the early 1900s, Grandpa Edgar and Grandma Lillian served in the Congo, deepest Africa, as Christian missionaries."

Gram resumed reading,

My Dear Mr. Johnston,

Your address was misplaced or you would have heard from me before now. I gave your clays the practical test especially. One of them, the real white, is a good type of kaolin and could be used in many forms of industrial arts. The darker one is a mixture of kaolin and common clay. Would make splendid jugs and the courser types of ceramic ware.

The very light gray is an excellent type of china clay —fires very pretty and works well on the wheel. These clays all have a varying commercial value. They would all make fancy bricks and tile. If your country is anything like ours, finding a market for them will be your hardest job.

With kindest regards to Mrs. Johnston.

Yours very sincerely,

TUSKEGEE NORMAL AND INDUSTRIAL INSTITUTE

FOUNDED BY BOOKER T. WASHINGTON

FOR THE TRAINING OF COLORED YOUNG MEN AND WOMEN

RESEARCH AND EXPERIMENT STATION
GEORGE W. CARVER, DIRECTOR

TUSKEGEE INSTITUTE, ALABAMA
Aug. 13 — 31.

My dear Mr. Johnston: —

Your address was misplaced or you
would have heard from me before now.
I gave your clays the practical test
especially. One of them, the real white is
a good type of kaolin, and could be
used in many forms of industrial
arts. The darker one is a mixture of
kaolin and common clay. Would make
splendid jugs and the coarser types of
ceramic ware.

The very light grey is an excellent type
of china clay fires very pretty and work
well on the wheel.

These clays all have a varying
commercial value, they would all make
sauces brick and tile.

Of your country is anything like ours,
finding a market for them will be your
hardest job. With kindest regards to Mrs.
Johnston. Yours very sincerely,

G. W. Carver.

She paused, and looked at Zach and Mags. "Now, try to read the signature."

They squinted, grimaced, and shook their heads in the negative. But then, Zach tried again, and suddenly, his eyes widened. Not only could he read the signature, but suddenly, crucial pieces of high school history were flooding back.

"*G.W. Carver.*" Zach started to smile, and his smile spread wider and wider. "No way. As in George Washington Carver, the famous professor and peanut guy?"

Gram was grinning from ear to ear. "Yes, that's right. The letter is from him." Zach and Mags' mouths dropped open in shock and disbelief. Zach reached carefully for the page of brittle letterhead. He cradled it carefully and stared in amazement at the piece of history he was holding in his palms.

"Yes, it's certainly for real," Gram replied. "Now how much do you know about him, beyond calling him the peanut guy?"

"I guess not much, really," Zach confessed. "I do remember that he discovered tons of uses for the peanut."

"That's right," Gram responded, "Actually, his role at Tuskegee involved teaching, writing, and researching. He came up with over three hundred products from the peanut, and one hundred eighteen from the sweet potato. But here's the best part, and it's very seldom reported in mainstream history books. He claimed to accomplish all of this because he worked with God in his laboratory. He affectionately called it 'God's Little Workshop.' George Carver sincerely believed that he was working with God in all that he did. One time in a speech he said, 'God is going to reveal to us things he never revealed before if we put our hands in his.'"

"So, I'm wondering," Mags jumped in with an excited question. "Do you think he was thinking that way, *I'm working with God,* on the day he tested the clay samples your grandfather sent from the Congo?"

"Oh, most definitely," Gram answered with confidence. "That's the kind of worker he was. His letters and speeches reveal it. Carver was one of those unique people who really lived his whole life in an extremely integrated way. Other quotes from his life show that he was very missional, working to serve others, for God's glory. Hold that thought—just a minute."

Moments later, Gram returned from her living room book-shelf and was paging through a thick Carver biography. Zach was pouring fresh hot water over three new tea bags. The story was just getting going. More tea was necessary.

"Here, take a listen to this," Gram invited. "In a letter to a Reverend Ward, Carver asked him: 'Pray for me please that every-thing said and done will be to his glory.' In another letter, this one to Robert Johnson, Carver reflects his personal satisfaction: 'Liv-ing for others is really the Christ life after all. Oh, the satisfaction, happiness and joy one gets out of it.' And when he was age sixty-three, Carver reflected his missional purpose: 'Man, who needed a purpose, a mission, to keep him alive, had one. He could be . . . God's coworker . . . My purpose alone must be God's purpose . . . as I worked on projects which fulfilled a real human need, forces were working through me which amazed me.'"

"Wow," Zach exclaimed. "'Almost sounds like Marshall talking about his mission field with Fords and their owners."

"Yes, yes, it does," Gram replied with a broad smile.

"So my Grandpa and Grandma Johnston had apparently met Carver on one of their furloughs," Gram explained. "Grandpa was curious about the clay samples, and we're pretty sure he was consid-ering a use for such clay, possibly as a business start-up there in the Congo. I have never seen my Grandfather's original letter that was sent to Carver, so I'm not sure what he described as his intentions for Carver running tests on the clay. But based on Carver's explana-tion in his reply letter, I've always conjectured that they were con-templating starting a business of making bricks or some brand of pottery works. Such business work would have gone hand-in-hand with their mission work, helping lift so many families to a stronger place economically. 'Would have been very redemptive!"

"Not unlike the guys from your church who are starting the construction business in Haiti, right?" Zach asked with affirming correlation. He explained further, "I think this concept of real busi-ness, for God's mission and glory, to bless others and advance the kingdom story—well, I just think it's an amazing concept."

"Yes, indeed it is," Gram affirmed. "And obviously, it's not a new concept with our current century. Back in the first century, the Apostle Paul and his coworkers, Priscilla and Aquilla, were tentmakers. Numerous missional endeavors have been grounded in serious business endeavors. It certainly seems, based on this letter, that my grandparents had espoused such thinking for the Congo. I'd imagine they fully anticipated that proceeds could bless local workers and their families, while also further funding new church sites across the region. 'Sad thing is, no one really knows for sure what Grandpa and Grandma did or did not do as a result of Carver's letter."

"That's OK, Gram," Zach consoled her, "I'm just loving such a connection from the family story. And I really dig the fact that from Carver's letter, we can pick up on their potential thinking toward business as mission. They apparently did not see them as exclusive of each other, but potentially, they saw the two, business and mission, going hand-in-hand. We all have a lot to learn from that story, and it's fascinating to see the domino effect. Across the decades, we're still talking about it today."

Mags suddenly sported a funny look on her face. "Wait a minute," she said with a feisty tone. "What in the world does any of this have to do with good old Henry Ford?"

"Oh my," Gram started laughing, "I nearly forgot. That's the fella with whom we started this conversation, didn't we?" Zach and Mags were nodding. "Well, open your iPad, and pull up *Google images*." The search box popped up. "Now just enter *Ford and Carver*."

Zach did, and the screen came to life with dozens of photos of the two men together.

"Whoa. They were buds!?" Mags half-asked, half-shouted, with wonder in her voice.

Gram chuckled. "You could say that. They spent some blocks of time working together on some special projects." Gram had a twinkle in her eye.

"You're not serious? This is amazing!" Zach had it. "They were working together on alternate fuels for the automobile, weren't they?"

"There you go. You've got it." Gram winked. "Now you've brought it full circle. Great job, Zach."

They sipped the last of their tea and called it a night. As he headed for bed, Zach was still shaking his head. *What stunning connections between work and mission across the decades,* Zach thought. *What a story God is still writing!*

Reflecting on Henry's Story, God's Story, and Your Story

1. Sharing with Gram about his grandfather's memorial service, Zach observes: "So many reflected how they knew Grandpa from his various business endeavors. Several of those guys shared that they follow Christ today because of Grandpa and Marshall eating breakfast with them over at the truck stop. It's very moving—all those people and their stories. Truly, Grandpa did amazing work for Christ's kingdom. He really did."

   What impresses you and challenges you from Zach's observation?

   How does this motivate you in your own relational cultivation?

   Who do you anticipate might show up for your funeral, and what might they say about your influence on their lives?

2. What do you learn from the author of the mystery letter?

How does George describe his life mission?

What impresses you about his view of his laboratory?

What might it mean for you to see your workplace like this? What could happen?

3. Evaluating his great great grandparents' perspective, Zach says: "They apparently did not see them as exclusive of each other, but potentially, they saw the two, business and mission, going hand-in-hand." What do you personally think of such an idea? How could you more effectively integrate, like Zach's great great grandparents did?

CHAPTER TEN

Groaning for Glory

Zach felt extra-rushed. It was Saturday morning, and they were supposed to meet up with Doc Ben midmorning—approximately 10:00 for coffee and lite breakfast. Now, it was already 9:15. Zach had been sitting at the Ohio Department of Motor Vehicles for forty-five minutes. *Come on, people!* Zach kept fuming inside, and his leg was jiggling out his impatience. Finally, out of nowhere, two more ODMV workers arrived at the counter and opened their stations. The crowd virtually cheered. Within a few minutes, Zach's number was called. He surrendered his little paper tag, and within a few more minutes, he had Henry's new registration and temporary tag. He rushed out the door and zoomed back to Gram's to pick up Maggie.

She was still chewing on a bagel with cream cheese and downing some coffee. "You know there will be coffee at the Clinton's, Mags. Come on. We *gotta* go." Zach was doing his best to pull her out the door. Doc Ben and his wife, Becky, had graciously invited Zach and Maggie to join them at their place on the edge of Granville. "We can make it by 10:00 sharp if we leave *right now*," Zach added with emphasis.

"OK, I'm coming. Did you get Henry's tags?" she asked.

Zach replied, "Yes, he's legal now."

"Oh, good," Maggie shot back. "He can go out to play in the neighborhood with all his other canine friends." Based on her veterinary world, Mags could not resist the humorous similarity between automotive tags and dog tags.

Zach rolled his eyes and groaned. "I can tell your coffee is kicking in, but you better be wittier than that with Doc Ben. Remember, he will have been up since five studying more Hebrew and Latin."

"Why do you think I've already guzzled two cups of coffee?" Mags volleyed. "Gotta be ready." She tossed her long, blond hair back in a band and grabbed a sweatshirt.

They headed out the door. "Skip the G37," Maggie instructed. "Let's take Henry. I'm in a vintage mood this morning."

Zach was hesitant. "I don't know. I don't think he's ready to go that far, and what if . . . "

"Skip the G37," Maggie instructed. "Let's take Henry. I'm in a vintage mood this morning." Zach was hesitant. "I don't know. I don't think he's ready to go that far, and what if . . ."

"Oh, come on, where's your sense of adventure, Sherlock Holmes?" Mags teased. "How can we know unless we try him out on the open road?" She jumped in the truck cab and slammed her door with an ornery smile.

Zach was shaking his head, but he played along. Five taps of the gas pedal, a turn of the key, and they headed for Granville. Henry was running surprisingly smooth. *At least the motor seems smooth,* Zach thought to himself. The body rattled and shook based on the wear and tear of almost four decades, and the exhaust was still rather loud. Zach and Maggie tried to talk, but gave up after a few minutes of shouting over the noisy tailpipes. Zach made sure to get in the last word. "Whose idea was this!?" Maggie just rolled her eyes and sat in silence, sulking for the rest of the ride.

They found Clinton's house number on the mailbox with no problem. Ben had warned them that they'd have to slow down along Church Street and watch for the box. Their house sat up a long lane, through a stretch of tall, thick trees.

Henry ascended the steep stretch of driveway. Once again, he seemed to be smiling through his round headlight eyes and wide-mouth bumper, as if to say, "Look at me. I got you here, didn't I?"

Zach was making instinctual, second-nature, architectural notes as they drove closer to the house. The Clinton's home was a classic two-story fusion of early American and Tudor lines. It was not large, but neither was it small. Zach's sense was, *'Just right for a former university professor and chaplain.*

Thick ivy vines graced the rock-covered chimney and cascaded around the edges of the side patio. The same historic Ohio fieldstone that composed the chimney flowed down and formed a half-wall 'round the beautiful, deck-like, side-of-house retreat. It had obviously been constructed many years before the pavers and TREX decks that had become so popular for outdoor motifs in recent decades. The whole patio included generous wicker seating, a gas grill, and abundant ferns and begonias. The Clintons waved a greeting from the patio and motioned for Mags and Zach to come up.

Zach brought Henry to a noisy stop, put him in park, and quickly switched off the key. He rumbled, sputtered, and finally fell silent. Zach could not help but feel embarrassed once again. He glared at Maggie, giving her the *whose idea was this* stare. She smiled back and proceeded to step from the truck with a ridiculous air of confidence. She ascended the rock steps to the patio like she was royalty. Zach followed along behind, just shaking his head. She was annoying and mesmerizing, all at the same time.

At the top of the steps, Ben and Becky met them with warm hugs and gracious greetings. The center glass table was overflowing with fresh blueberry muffins, a variety of other pastries, and, of course, carafes filled with flavored coffees.

"You're expecting other guests?" Zach wondered. "This is opulent. What a spread!"

"Oh, no," Ben reassured him. "Becky just loves to entertain, and she can't seem to prep for any group smaller than ten. So the four of us will have to suffer through this morning with enough to feed fifty." Becky attempted to explain herself, but everyone proceeded to just tease her more.

"So that's the Ford pickup your grandpa gave you?" Ben asked with a grin.

"Yea," Zach responded sheepishly. "Not exactly the sleek sportster that normally traffics roads in your neighborhood. Sorry for the noise. *Someone insisted* we drive it." Zach threw eye darts in Maggie's direction.

She proceeded to enthusiastically explain how Zach had just gotten the registration and plates that morning, as well as how much work Marshall had already done to make Henry roadworthy again. It was evident to Zach that Mags was in love with Henry. That much was certain.

"That's great!" Doc Ben said with a genuine, congratulatory tone. "He looks like a solid old classic, capable of being further restored in the years to come. Your Grandpa knew vehicles quite well, and Marshall certainly knows Fords. If they both saw potential in a piece, you can feel pretty good about it."

Zach was feeling a bit better with such reassuring acceptance. *OK, so maybe he doesn't think the rednecks just invaded his neighborhood, after all,* Zach thought to himself.

"It's always neat to realize how things can be reclaimed, reinvented, restored, and redeemed," Doc stated with real conviction. Mags and Zach could tell he was merging the conversation and now speaking with some metaphorical sense. They both smiled. By now, they had all poured large mugs of coffee, mixed in their favorite creamer flavors, and plucked several delectable muffins from the luxurious spread. Becky smiled with satisfaction as the four of them began to indulge. She was fully in her element.

> "We all need to be rescued, redeemed, and remade, a lot like this old pickup. All along the way, God has been working to accomplish that, and he invites us to join him in his work, in the story he is unfolding."

Ben continued in his own work element, now with sensitive, thoughtful focus. "It's certainly fun to realize how this truck pictures God's redeeming work, and even the glory to come. This is right at the heart of his missional story, to seek, reach, and transform people, from dented-up, broken-down, marred by sin, and helpless. We all need to be rescued, redeemed, and remade, a lot like this old pickup. All along the way, God has been working to accomplish that, and he invites us to join him in his work, in the story he is unfolding."

"Yes, yes!" Zach agreed enthusiastically, "and that's the same correlation Marshall made a couple weeks back, that first time we talked with him. I have to tell you, Doc, throughout all of these days while I've been home, I feel as if God has sent me to a boot camp on my attitudes and actions at work. He's really been working me over inside, almost like one very big therapy session."

Doc Ben chuckled and nodded. Then he added, "Well, when you're receptive, reflective, and willing to grow in self-awareness, you're primed and ready to let God work in new ways in your life. Then, and it seems like *only then,* you are ready to start joining him at work in new ways."

Zach was nodding. "Yes, and several big themes have kept emerging for me. First, I've been seeing the importance of recognizing that I *do* indeed have an important role to play in God's story, and that must involve my role at work. Right there at work, it can be and should be *my mission field* every day. And that's true for all of us. We are called by God—every disciple is called—and he commissions us to join his mission. In fact, this is all part of the restoration of his original plans from back at Creation. This is part and parcel of . . . oh, shoot, what do you call them? You know, the Latin phrases . . ."

Mags chimed in with a grin. "The *imago Dei* and the *missio Dei.*"

"Thanks, star student," Zach affirmed with a cynical glare. "And, then I've also noticed, undergirding all of this is a fully integrated perspective, a holistic view of one's life. People who get this, I mean *really* get this missional thing, they seem to deliberately resist compartmentalizing their lives. They don't see themselves as having a secular life and then a separate, sacred life."

"And they don't view themselves as *going* to church on Sunday," Mags added, "and then having a separate work life on Monday through Saturday." The other three were smiling and nodding in passionate agreement. "Instead," Mags continued, " They are *being* the church all week long. And they certainly don't carve some deep division between ordained clergy and ordinary laity. Every Christian serves as a priest in God's kingdom. Yes, there are leaders who have their leading roles, but they are not more sacred, more called, or more ordained than other priests in the kingdom."

"Amen, sister," Becky cheered. "Years ago, I had my own internal battle with feeling inferior and inadequate. Ben was amazing at teaching, preaching, researching, and leading others. It seems like I was always just cooking, baking, and otherwise preparing to host groups of people, so he could do his ministry stuff. I'm really good at doing all the preparation. I love creativity in the kitchen, and I sense the smile of God when I do it, but then there was always this nagging feeling. You know, the voices inside saying, 'Yes, but that's not the sacred, contemplative work. It's the active, lower, everyday, earthy stuff.' I did a lot of discussing this with friends and with Ben, plus I had to be open to that work of God inside my heart. Finally, I realized, and I still have to keep realizing, that when I do my serving for God's glory, I am indeed living out his mission and advancing his kingdom."

Zach concurred, "That's really good, and I'm sensing similar shifts in my own thinking about my work as an architect."

Zach continued recounting his journey. "The third big theme for me—and this has been *huge*—is the way missional workers are constantly cultivating stronger relationships with people in their sphere who need to experience Christ's gracious salvation. I see how you're doing that at the hospital, Doc. My Grandpa did it with Marshall and other guys at the Buckeye Lake Truck Stop. Grandma tells about all the people at your church who are praying for others, caring for others, and sharing Christ with others in and through their jobs. And then there are the business leaders who are starting new businesses with a missional thrust, like those guys doing the residential construction company in Haiti. Again, and again, it seems like it's all about building real, caring, authentic relationships with others, for Christ's glory.

"Right on, Zach," Doc Ben affirmed. "And these kingdom-focused, relationally-focused business startups are not unique to our church right here. More and more, they are springing up with great momentum all over the place. Why, I believe right there in your area of Pennsylvania is *Hope International,* a growing micro-finance initiative that helps people all over the world start new business initiatives with small loans. There's also a dynamic business called *Ten Thousand Villages,* which for decades now has been cultivating global trading relationships."

Becky chimed in. "I absolutely love *Ten Thousand Villages!* Their inventory is always beautiful. Artisans all over the world receive a fair price for their work and consumers have access to distinctive handcrafted items. They seek to establish long-term buying relationships in places where skilled artisans are under- or unemployed, and in which they lack other opportunities for income. So, they bless needy families and help grow regional economies in needy places around the globe."

"There are coffee businesses with a kingdom agenda." Doc Ben lifted his mug in a grand toast. "And there are also English-teaching, skill-cultivating schools and missional ice cream vendors, and there are . . . well, the list could go on and on. It's really amazing how God is at work all over the world through vibrant business initiatives. And he's using bright, big-hearted, business-minded people to create such kingdom endeavors."

Zach put his hand in the air, as if calling a timeout. "OK, yes, I'm enthused by all of this, and I am personally committing to explore more about the construction company starting in Haiti. I really sense maybe I could participate somehow there. We'll see. But I have at least

"I really want to know: Can my daily work as an architect count for something? And I mean really count, beyond simply being instrumental in supplying tithes and offerings, or even just instrumental in providing a sort of stage, a platform for evangelizing people who need Christ."

one remaining question. You might even say it's a *burning* question, both metaphorically and literally. You'll see why in a moment. I really want to know: Can my daily work as an architect count for something? And I mean *really* count, beyond simply being instrumental in supplying tithes and offerings, or even just instrumental in providing a sort of stage, a platform for evangelizing people who need Christ."

"That is a phenomenal question, Zach." Doc Ben was beaming from ear to ear. "Truly exceptional!"

"Now *you* are the star student," Mags teased and patted him on the head. "What a good boy." For some reason, he now felt like a golden retriever.

"This is so important to grasp for all of us, if we are going to live a genuine, missional life," Ben said with real conviction. "You'll have to deeply consider this on your own and arrive at your own conclusion. But I personally have come to believe the answer is a resounding *yes!* I believe that based on God's original intention for creation to involve healthy, creative work . . . and based on our being coworkers and co-reigning with him, it is his intention to redeem our work, to restore the intrinsic value of our everyday work. So, when we rule and reign, when we give creative, solid, strategic leadership in our world, we are helping restore that original creation intention. Our work can indeed glorify God and take on lasting significance."

Zach was listening intently, and occasionally ran his fingers through his hair. Of course, Mags noticed and couldn't help but think the curls were especially thick and wavy today.

"I believe Jesus' own resurrection helps us toward understanding this." Doc continued. Mags and Zach both gave Ben confused looks.

"Now hold on. Follow close. I believe this is some of what Paul is aiming toward in 1 Corinthians 15, when he describes Jesus' own resurrection in a body that is both physical and glorified. He insists that Jesus' resurrection is a first, a foretaste of more to come, pointing to other very physical, tangible components of the redemption glory that's coming. In that same chapter, Paul describes our own human resurrection, including new bodies, but they will not be ethereal spirits. At the resurrection, we get spiritual bodies, like Christ's, but we're not simply silhouettes. Our new bodies will also have actual physical qualities."

Again, Zach gave a curious look. "Watch this," Doc continued. "You might remember that Luke, in chapter twenty-four of his

Gospel, describes Jesus as walking, speaking, breaking bread, eating fish, displaying flesh and bones with scars in his hands and feet, as well as accomplishing other very tangible, physical things. So I have conjectured, along with many other thinkers across the years: If the earthly bodies we originally had will be brought back together and glorified (and we have the promise that will happen), is it not also possible for God to someday bring back together certain tangible elements from all of creation, including redemptive results of our work we performed across the years? In fact, as a concluding command at the end of 1 Corinthians 15, look at what Paul says."

Ben had his iPad handy and he scrolled to verse fifty-eight in the New Living Translation. He read aloud: "So, my dear brothers and sisters, be strong and immovable. Always work enthusiastically for the Lord, for you know that nothing you do for the Lord is ever useless."

Zach and Mags were both shaking their heads in amazement. "I've simply never really considered that verse in its context before," Zach exclaimed. "What a call to a purposeful, integrated life at work!"

"Absolutely!" Ben affirmed with enthusiasm. And this matches up with what Paul says in Romans 8. When we met at Dunkin's the week before last, we scratched the surface on that scripture spot. Remember, all the creation is groaning in anticipation of the glory to come."

Zach jumped there on his Bible App on his phone. "Here we go. Verse eighteen in the NLT: 'Yet what we suffer now is nothing compared to the glory he will reveal to us later. For all creation is waiting eagerly for that future day when God will reveal who his children really are . . .' Zach scanned a moment and jumped to verse twenty-one. 'The creation looks forward to the day when it will join God's children in glorious freedom from death and decay. For we know that all creation has been groaning as in the pains of childbirth right up to the present time. And we believers also groan, even though we have the Holy Spirit within us as a foretaste of future glory, for we long for our bodies to be released from sin and suffering.' Does that give us the overview?" Zach asked.

That's great," Doc affirmed. "And did you catch the glory?"

Mags couldn't hold back. "I *get* it! With all of this groaning in suffering, both for people and all of creation, including our work, we're constantly reminded of sin's curse. But there's glory yet to come. In faith, we anticipate what's yet to come. And God's work in this world, the story he is writing, is all moving toward that transforming, life-changing work. And yes, it's undeniable. Paul sees this as having actual, tangible results in the physical creation." She paused and then added, "I think this *has* to include our work results, since he originally planned for us to accomplish meaningful work. Why, if he intends to redeem his good creation . . . why would he not renew and restore at least some of our everyday work as part of that glory to come?"

> *"Mags couldn't hold back. "I get it! With all of this groaning in suffering, both for people and all of creation, including our work, we're constantly reminded of sin's curse. But there's glory yet to come. In faith, we anticipate what's yet to come. And God's work in this world, the story he is writing, is all moving toward that transforming, life-changing work."*

All three of her coffee comrades were nodding in agreement. And Ben added, "Many Bible scholars refer to our current kingdom status today as living in the *already, not yet* of God's kingdom story. Because Christ has come, he has *already* inaugurated the kingdom, and we can indeed taste some likeness of the redemption. Christ's own great works, his miracles, and even our good works and outcomes today, are genuine, tangible tastes of the kingdom. And still, we realize these are but previews of more glory to come."

"So," Zach was leaning back in, "perhaps several of my buildings, maybe a couple of the very best ones that really make God smile, just maybe they might be redeemed, renewed, and restored in the end."

"*May be*, Zach." Doc Ben was grinning. "I'm serious, it may very well be. And not just the church buildings and mission hospitals, as grand as those can be." Zach laughed and faked a look of relief.

Ben continued, "I have a hunch the same God who was so crazy-creative to design the cosmos can delight in other brilliant designs by his coworkers, like you and me. And after all, Revelation reveals that when Christ sets up his final kingdom with the new heavens and new earth, we will be in a new kind of Garden City, the New Jerusalem. It appears this will include original components of Eden, plus new components of a marvelously impressive city with real walls and real buildings. And there will still be even more good work to accomplish."

"Alright," Zach said, "but here's my burning question, and it's a big one. I grew up being taught that everything is going to burn up at the final judgment day. Everything physical is temporal. This world is not our home, and so only what's spiritual really matters. All the material things of this world, including automobiles and architecture, trees and tulips, are doomed to destruction. If my memory serves me correctly, I think this idea came from Peter."

"That's right," Ben replied. "Peter's words in 2 Peter 3:10. Many people think he says that everything will be devastated, totally burned up and vanish. OK, ready for some more Latin?" Doc asked with professorial excitement.

"Yes!" Mags enthusiastically answered. Zach rolled his eyes.

Ben continued. "The idea you are referencing is known as *annihilatio mundi*. This view teaches that the world will be annihilated and a totally new one created. Since the results of all humankind's work throughout history will supposedly be obliterated in the final apocalyptic catastrophe, human work then holds no direct ultimate significance. So, just as you recognize, based on this perspective, the present creation and all cultural work do not hold intrinsic value beyond some spiritual, sanctifying benefit to people's souls. Any value is only secondary and supporting."

"Exactly!" Zach exclaimed. "This thinking, logically followed out, should actually motivate me to quit my design work in order to serve in some other more direct, spiritual work that holds primary importance. If all my work on building designs, and then the buildings themselves, if all they really serve to do is create environments for the *real* work, the spiritual mission, to be accomplished in people's lives, then what's the long-term point? They're just going to burn up in the end. So if I really want to work on what will truly last, then I should more closely align my focus and energy with God's mission of saving souls, focusing on the deeper, more spiritual matters in people's lives. I guess at the very least, I should only design and build church buildings and mission clinics." Zach was reasoning, but with sprinkles of vibrant sarcasm.

Ben and Becky were both grinning. "You've nailed it, Zach," Ben affirmed. "And many a business person or other marketplace Christian has left his original vocation based on this very logic, motivated by such a call to *what matters most.*"

"Sometimes," Becky added, "a change in someone's field *is* indeed appropriate because there is a new stirring, a fresh prompting from God for a new avenue of service. Or, perhaps a person has made fresh discoveries regarding her or his God-given gifts, talents, and passions. But honestly, too often such a switch only lands a person in a place of frustration and lack of fruitfulness, all because they are not really serving out of their God-given gifts, passions, and talents. It would be like if I decided I should no longer bake and host, but instead start teaching, leading, and writing, like Ben does. After all, obviously what he does, well, *that's more spiritual and will have eternal, lasting results.* Honestly, I would be dismally ineffective."

"To say nothing of how much we'd miss the coffee and pastries," Zach interjected. Everyone concurred with laughter, and they saw it as a great segue for refills.

Reflecting on Henry's Story, God's Story, and Your Story

1. What is Doc Ben saying when he compares Henry's condition with the redemptive story God is unfolding?

2. What are Zach's three big themes?

   Which of the three proves to be most challenging and stretching to your attitudes and actions? Why?

   In which one of the three are you experiencing some real progress and personal change? Explain.

3. Do you resonate with Zach's big question about the eternal value of his daily work? He asks: "Can my daily work as an architect count for something? And I mean *really* count, beyond simply being instrumental in supplying tithes and offerings, or even just instrumental in providing a sort of stage, a platform for evangelizing people who need Christ."

   What are your own thoughts in reply?

4. Doc Ben makes a big deal about Romans 8. Explore this passage on your own.

   What are your biggest observations about redemption and glory? (vs. 18–21)

5. What do you think about Doc's proposition that some of our daily work and work's outcomes, like Zach's buildings, might be redeemed along with the rest of creation? Agree or disagree? Why?

6. Evaluate, pray, and make some fresh plans for relational cultivation with coworkers, clients, or other work contacts this week. Celebrate progress, those points where you see God at work and using you to work in others' lives for his glory. Give him praise!

CHAPTER ELEVEN

Whatever

Stirring his fresh cup of java, Doc Ben continued. "*Annihila-tio mundi* is only one view, and I would propose, along with a couple of my good friends who have indeed done their heavy homework, that the alternate view is much stronger. *Transformatio mundi* maintains that the final judgment will bring about transformation for creation, not annihilation and total replacement. This is grounded in what we've already discussed from Romans 8 about humans, creation, and the Spirit groaning with anticipation for coming glory, plus the visions of new creation in Revelation 21 and 22. *All things become new!*"

Zach broke in and challenged, "OK, but can we just ignore Peter?"

"Not on your life," Ben reassured with gusto. "We should read Peter more carefully. A couple of my scholar friends maintain that 2 Peter 3:10–13 is not best read in an annihilationist manner. The judgment will indeed penetrate the elemental depths of material existence, with the goal of destroying all the sin that permeated the fabric of creation and that would prevent it from becoming genuinely new. But the most reliable Greek manuscripts suggest that the earth and everything in it will be *laid bare*. That's a stronger translation and interpretation. This judgment then purges this earth and everything in it, instead of replacing it."

"Sounds like a powerful cleansing that makes way for renewal," Zach synthesized.

Mags was grinning and laughing. "Sorry for my lower-level, down-to-earth frivolity. Yes, with that comment, I'm compartmentalizing with my deep-seated, Platonic roots. But with my mind's eye, as I hear you saying this, I'm replaying the climactic scene from the old movie *Lion King*. Do you remember?" All three were nodding.

With dramatic flair, Mags stood up and rehearsed the scene. "The evil lion, Scar, and his demonic hyena friends ruined the lush grasslands and the paradise of Pride Rock. Toward the very end, the region catches fire and seems to burn up. But then, refreshing rain falls and new life springs up, and all is renewed. The fire in that scene provided a purging, a cleansing preparation toward everything becoming beautiful and renewed once again!"

> *"But then, refreshing rain falls and new life springs up, and all is renewed. The fire in that scene provided a purging, a cleansing preparation toward everything becoming beautiful and renewed once again!"*

With big smiles, all three audience members broke into applause. Mags pretended to curtsy. "Don't mock me too much, but I've actually cried a number of times at the climax of this scene." She sat down.

Doc affirmed, "That's a very good illustration, Miss Maggie. We certainly wouldn't want to build our future-thinking theology on a movie, but such a colorful, big screen story from classic movie culture probably echoes the essence of what God will do in his own grand story better than any other. Oh, and by the way, don't forget, who was instrumental in helping restore Pride Rock? Who had to take his role seriously and work toward change?"

"Simba, of course!" Mags answered.

"Yes," Ben affirmed, "The heir to the kingdom, son of Mufasa. At a very pivotal point, way before the fire-and-transformation climax you've referenced, Simba is wrestling with his own life's purpose. And he only gets motivated to play his role in the story by looking at his reflection in the water. Do you remember? He ends up seeing his father's own face. So, his turning point was remembering that he carried his father's image. He was destined to be the Lion King, and that personal epiphany motivates him to actually go work to make a difference."

"*Imago Dei* leads to *missio Dei!*" Zach correlated with great gusto.

"Exactly!" Ben said. "So, with *transformatio mundi*, God renews the original creation he had dubbed as *very good*, and he works to transform, heal, and restore the ground and the things on the ground. God's purposes for humans and the rest of creation will be realized once and for all. And the ancient prophecies more than imply that such restoration will include ultimate creativity for new culture making. The prophet Isaiah, in Isaiah 65:21-22, describes the literal new heavens and new earth. The scene includes houses being built for people to live in them, vineyards being planted and their fruit being eaten, and God's people being able to *enjoy the work of their hands.* And all of this will be enjoyed by people from all the nations who have responded to God's missional love, repented of their sins, and become coworkers in Christ's kingdom once again."

> "Wow!" Zach exclaimed. "This view really lifts our daily work to an extraordinary level. It helps everyone know that they have important work to accomplish. With this perspective, any work that matches biblical ethics and Christ-honoring values can be done to serve other people, for God's glory."

"Wow!" Zach exclaimed. "This view really lifts our daily work to an extraordinary level. It helps everyone know that they have important work to accomplish. With this perspective, any work that matches biblical ethics and Christ-honoring values can be done to serve other people, for God's glory."

Mags was staring at Zach intently. He had started running his fingers through his hair with a vengeance. *What a predictable, quirky tick,* she thought. *Yes, it's a cute tick, but I know exactly what's just below the surface of his psyche at this very moment.*

So, she just blurted it out. "Tell him, Zach. Tell him about Uncle Clyde's infamous quotation." Zach hung his head. She was striking at his emotional-familial Achilles heel. "Go ahead, tell Doc and Becky," she prodded.

Everyone was quiet. Zach just stared into nowhere, and then he realized that everyone was waiting for him to speak. It was an awkward silence. He adjusted himself in his seat, clasped his hands, wrinkled his nose, and fixed his eyes on Doc Ben. With a paced cadence in his voice, he stated it: *"Only one life, 'twill soon be past, only what's done for Christ will last.* That's what he says." It was stated with a blend of sarcasm and a slight hint of bitterness. "He's said it to me off and on ever since I was young. He frequently adds an explanatory comment, such as, 'Make sure you make your life truly count, Son.' And yes, in case you can't tell, I find it so annoying and belittling." Zach looked away again.

Ben waited a moment, and then with thoughtfulness in his voice and a soft tone, he offered some perspective. "I know *of* your uncle, Zach, but I don't really know him. For what it's worth, I'm guessing he means well. And I'm also guessing there's a part of your heart that would really like to have his approval." It was a statement entwined with a serious question.

"Yes, I suppose so," Zach answered. "And I suppose I know why." He sighed and continued. "For big portions of my boyhood years, his voice and views held a major influence in my spiritual nurture, as my family visited the Chapel often for services. Plus, Uncle Clyde took me fishing and showed some genuine interest in me."

"That makes total sense," Ben interjected. "As a grown adult, you still want his approval. 'Very normal."

Zach continued, "But throughout the years, as I grew more independent and more focused on my love for design work, he seemed to grow more judgmental of my vocational intentions. Numerous times, he more than implied that he and my aunt were praying for me to surrender to God's call to be a pastor or missionary, to *truly* enter the Lord's work."

"Hmm. That's sad, but also typical." Ben said with a frown. "Just a couple thoughts that might help you," he offered. Zach gave a receptive nod. "First, your uncle's behavior is predictable of some-one living out the compartmentalized life. 'Truth is, while his poem sounds noble and it is probably well-intentioned, his interpretation, such lack of holistic integration, has significantly limited his own life and ministry. It's time you just call that what it is, deep within your own heart."

"I get that," Zach concurred. "I need to frame it better in my own psyche, not let him get under my skin so easily. I try. I really do, and those times I think that way, I have better peace. Really."

Doc continued. "Old paradigms are hard to give up. He's not likely to easily alter his view. It *could* happen, but only if he hits a personal crisis or transition point that makes him remarkably open to a shift in perspective, a serious change. Again, that *could* happen. People can change. But you have to realize, it's not your job to *make* that happen. And even more important, you have to decide to stop linking your own sense of life fulfillment to your uncle's approval or disapproval."

A look of slight relief came over Zach's face. "That does help. 'Helps me frame it different. And I guess I need to remember that and replay those thoughts more often."

"Yes, it's all part of renewing your inner thinking. Realize that Uncle Clyde's haunting assessment for you has been stirred afresh and anew because of your Grandpa's death and such close proxim-ity to family during these weeks. These kinds of feelings take some time to think through, pray through, talk through, and work out in healthier ways. Give it time."

Zach was nodding in agreement. "I will. Sincerely, thank you."

"Oh, and one other thing," Doc Ben continued. "I know it feels tainted for you, but the poem itself can actually be a good motiva-tion, if you think about it." Zach frowned and tilted his head.

Doc continued, "It was written by a missionary named C.T. Studd. Studd served Christ on several different continents during the late nineteenth and early twentieth centuries. He was very de-voted and very influential. Try your best to separate the poem from Preacher Clyde's guilt-layered implications toward you personally. Instead, think about it in light of Paul's encouragement in Colos-sians 3:23-24: *Whatever you do, work at it with all your heart, as working for the Lord, not for human masters, since you know that you will receive an inheritance from the Lord as a reward. It is the Lord Christ you are serving."*

A look of fresh perspective came across Zach's face.

"Just like you've been discovering," Ben continued, "your own *whatever* can include designing great architecture, Zach. And your *whatever*, Maggie, can include phenomenal pet care. Work at it with all your heart, as working for the Lord. Always remember, in everything you do, you are serving for his glory, to make him more and more famous! Every person can serve for his glory in their *whatever* work."

> *"And your* whatever, Maggie, *can include phenomenal pet care. Work at it with all your heart, as working for the Lord. Always remember, in everything you do, you are serving for his glory, to make him more and more famous! Every person can serve for his glory in their* whatever *work."*

All of a sudden, Maggie realized it was nearly 1 p.m. They had been drinking coffee and talking up a storm for almost three hours. All four agreed, the time had flown, the conversation had been rich, and Becky's pastries had been especially scrumptious. Zach and Mags expressed great gratitude, exchanged hugs, and headed down the stone steps toward Henry. Ben and Becky trailed behind them to say goodbye.

Zach got the old fella started. Mags jumped in and slammed her door. The exhaust rumbled and Henry performed his typical shakes and sputters as he was warming up.

"Really something, isn't it!?" Zach shouted with an air of cynicism through his open window.

"He's *something* alright!" Doc shouted back. "I like him. All that noise, the rumbling and rattling, I think it's pretty special. If you ask me, 'seems like it's just his own special way of groaning in anticipation of the glorious redemption yet to come." Everyone laughed.

"That's certainly a more positive way to frame it," Zach affirmed. "He's a piece of work, that's for sure. Thanks again. See you soon."

As they descended the Clinton's drive, there was a sharp curve toward the final approach to the road's edge. Zach misjudged how quickly they were approaching the road, and he had to throw on the brakes. Just in time, Henry came to a sudden stop right next to the mailbox, but the slant of the driveway and jolt of the new brakes sent Mags sliding across the bench seat in Zach's direction. She landed right next to him.

"Whoa, sorry for the scary stop, Mags," Zach replied with great sincerity.

She raised a fist and pounded him on the shoulder. "Sure you are!" But she stayed put, shoulder-to-shoulder, *so very close.* And Zach grinned inside.

Reflecting on Henry's Story, God's Story, and Your Story

1. What's the difference between *annihilatio mundi* and *transformatio mundi*?

2. Explore for yourself 2 Peter 3:10–13 as well as Isaiah 65:17–25.

   How have you understood the 2 Peter passage in the past? Do you think everything will be burned up and replaced, or will it be cleansed and purged?

   What difference does it make to the value of your daily work and work's outcomes?

What impresses you about the description of new heavens and new earth in Isaiah 65? What do you learn about work's role?

3. How does Doc Ben help Zach process Uncle Clyde's poem and personal evaluation of Zach's life work? What's truly helpful? What might you add by way of counsel for Zach?

4. Read Colossians 3:23–24 several times again. What stands out to you now, in light of all you have been learning and experiencing? How does this impact your own *whatever*?

5. How are you praying and planning to bless other coworkers, clients, or business contacts this week? How is relational cultivation progressing with your original several friends at work? Are you seeing opportunities to answer questions or share your faith story based on piqued curiosity? Have you offered prayer for a need or offered serving help to someone this week?

CHAPTER TWELVE

Glorious New Lines

B ack at Gram's, they parked Henry right behind the G37, at the edge of the drive like normal, so as not to block her Honda CR-V inside the garage. Zach backed Henry into his spot. Anytime, anywhere Zach parked, he always backed the vehicle into place. "Makes for a quick getaway." Whether it truly saved time or not, that was always his explanation.

Once inside, they rehearsed for Gram their morning's conversation with the Clintons. As they were talking with Gram, a thunderstorm appeared to be rolling in. Thick, gray clouds were gathering, and the tops of the trees were starting to sway. Gram had an eye on the storm brewing out the back window, and she was also listening attentively as they told her what they had learned. She always thrilled at soaking up fresh intellectual concepts that held potential for big life change.

Zach explained, "So much of what we discussed this morning supplies a poignant synthesis of my ideas and heart stirrings. Knowing confidently that my mission field is my workplace, integrating my faith every day in all I am and all I do, and seeking to very intentionally cultivate caring, praying, sharing relationships with others—all for the glory of Christ. These are truly revolutionary concepts for me!"

Gram was grinning and nodding her head.

Zach continued, "I am truly amazed at what I sense God is developing in my thinking. And I have fresh resolve toward fresh action. I'm very serious, Gram. These several weeks have been incredible! It's been deeply sad and hard to say goodbye to Grandpa, and yet I feel like God has been using all of these events, along with people like the Clintons, plus Marshall, and certainly you, in order to help me arrive at a better place in how I view and pursue my life mission through work."

"Knowing confidently that my mission field is my workplace, integrating my faith every day in all I am and all I do, and seeking to very intentionally cultivate caring, praying, sharing relationships with others—all for the glory of Christ. These are truly revolutionary concepts for me!"

"That's wonderful," Gram affirmed. "I know your grandfather had become so passionate about living an intentionally missional life. I'm confident he'd be thrilled to know that all of the circumstances and people have been working together to accomplish good plans for your life." A thoughtful look came over her face. "'Sounds a lot like what Paul says in Romans 8, 'that in all things God works for the good of those who love him.' And it's powerful to remember that this *good* God intends for us, according to verse twenty-nine, is to be *conformed to the image of his Son*."

"And why shouldn't it surprise me," Zach reflected, "that we're talking about Romans 8 and the image of God again?!"

Mags added, "Are you going to tell her about Doc Ben's coaching you on Uncle Clyde's poem?"

Zach proceeded to explain about Ben's encouragement in how to better handle his emotions and his own sense of fulfillment in the face of Uncle Clyde's approval or disapproval. He also told her about Ben's better take on C.T. Studd's witty rhyme.

"C.T. Studd." Gram repeated the name with a sense of recognition and remembrance. "That's right. Same era as your great great grandparents. If my memory serves me correctly, Studd also spent some time in the Congo. I am not certain if their paths ever crossed, but they certainly would have been there in the same span of years."

"Is that right?" Zach asked. "Amazing."

"Yes, and you might find this interesting," Gram continued. "Most everyone on the global missions scene of that day was impacted in some way by the vibrant example of one leading character. Our family history relates that Grandma Lillian and Grandpa Edgar had been heavily influenced by the life and thinking of David Livingstone, the famous missions pioneer. Oh, you have to hear this."

Grandma disappeared for a moment, but quickly returned with another tome in hand. She still had the Carver biography sitting there on the edge of the kitchen table from their previous late night conversation. With a tone of excited discovery, she said, "Here's one of Livingstone's leading thoughts, shared in a Cambridge University speech in 1857."

> In going back to that country, my object is to open up traffic along the banks of the Zambesi, and also to preach the gospel. The natives of Central Africa are very desirous of trading, but their only traffic is at present in slaves, of which the poorer people have an unmitigated horror: it is therefore most desirable to encourage the former principle, and thus open a way for the consumption of free productions, and the introduction of Christianity and commerce. By encouraging the native propensity for trade, the advantages that might be derived in a commercial point of view are incalculable; nor should we lose sight of the inestimable blessings it is in our power to bestow upon the unenlightened African, by giving him the light of Christianity. Those two pioneers of civilization—Christianity and commerce—should ever be inseparable.

Zach raised his eyebrows, as he supplied correlating commentary: "That is a stunning statement of integration. Livingstone obviously did not espouse a divided life, the sacred-secular split. Instead, he viewed life holistically, with spiritual mission and business going hand-in-hand." Zach was running his fingers back through his thick curls as he reflected. Mags was grinning. *There it is again.* She knew he was thinking oh-so-deeply about the personal ramifications for his own sense of calling, mission, and effectiveness at work.

Zach continued, "It just seems, the more and more I think on this, that if this concept holds such biblical grounding as well as practical precedent from leaders across the decades, even across centuries of history, well, it seems like more of us should embrace such thinking as present-day leaders in our workplaces."

"I agree," Gram responded. "This seems like one of those areas that *should* be so obvious. The majority of people spend oodles of hours at work, but in all of our compartmentalized thinking, we've missed it. For me, as Pastor Tom started emphasizing these missional concepts throughout our church and helping us mobilize as a congregation to really *be* the church in our workplaces every day, it proved revolutionary for my work with students and coworkers over at school, before I retired. Honestly, I already enjoyed my job, at least most days." Gram laughed.

> *"And I'll even grab some lunches and coffee breaks, very intentionally, with kingdom purposes in mind. I want to start to get to know what's going on in their lives, beyond work, so I am able to see how God is already working in their lives. I want to be able to pray for them, encourage them, and care for them and their families. Along the way, as they see I genuinely care, I believe this will pique their curiosity."*

She further explained, "Mind you, I already held some of these ideas in my personal framework through reading and correlating I had done across the years. But with some refocus and personal intentionality, I found myself having a greater influence and greater sense of effectiveness in my mission. It became a real adventure to actually join God at work in what he was already accomplishing in people's lives. And it proved life-changing, both for others and for me."

"That's truly awesome, Gram," Zach affirmed. "I know I'm going back to work with that new focus and a couple personal action goals. Much like Grandpa and Marshall have done over the years, I'm setting a goal to eat two to three breakfasts with coworkers and clients each week. And I'll even grab some lunches and coffee breaks, very intentionally, with kingdom purposes in mind. I want to start to get to know what's going on in their lives, beyond work, so I am able to see how God is already working in their lives. I want to be able to pray for them, encourage them, and care for them and their families. Along the way, as they see I genuinely care, I believe this will pique their curiosity. They'll ask questions, just like Marshall started to ask Grandpa, and just like your students and coworkers asked you big questions."

"That's right!" Gram was nodding and affirming.

Zach continued. "And I plan to be ready to answer those questions and share the message of Christ, a step at a time, and to help them trust him and grow as his disciples. But I realize that such sharing has to start with my intentionally caring. I *have* to spend more time with them in order to do that effectively."

Maggie volunteered with real spunk, "Ditto for me! I'm going to move beyond loving pets and just tolerating pet owners. I know people are still going to irritate me, but with God's love and grace changing me, I'm committing to really connect with people out of genuine, Christ-honoring love. Do you know something that hit me like a truckload of bricks the other day?"

Mags paused, took a serious breath, and she continued. "Our mobile offices perform, on average, ten euthanasia procedures each week. That means typically, my team of vets and I have some level of interaction with about ten pet owners and their families who are grieving the loss of their beloved furry friend. In the past, I've just expressed a simple *deeply sorry for your loss* comment, and I've quickly moved on with my day. If we happen to be on top of our game, we've sent out the token sympathy cards. But honestly, more often than not, we don't. It's been hitting me that one of the most Christ-like things I could do with those clients is to slow down enough to really demonstrate that I care. As I see further openness, I can offer prayer, and I can do a follow-up phone call to check on them. I can certainly insist that my staff sends out the sympathy cards in a timely, heartfelt, truly caring manner. That's just good values, respecting people's emotions, and showing we truly care."

"That's seriously good!" Zach exclaimed. And without even thinking, he grabbed for her hand. She blushed, grinned, and held his hand tight in return. Her words were indeed impressively thoughtful, practical, caring, and intentional toward vibrant relational mission.

"Oh, and one other action goal for me," Zach proclaimed. "I already called Jason, the leader with the *Homes for Haiti* team from your church. Thanks for giving me his number. 'Found out, they're having a next steps planning meeting in mid-July, and he said I'm welcome to come. So I'm going to zoom back over. Then, I'll likely take info back and start talking with other guys at the firm. We have enough downtime right now. I was actually thinking, *Perhaps this is God's perfect timing for us to make a global investment as a firm? What if this is God's way of nudging us in some new directions?* We'll see!"

Gram grinned and said, "This is all very good work you kids are aiming to accomplish. Just make sure you're doing it all for Christ, for his kingdom, for his glory. Never forget that. It's for his glory."

"Hey!" Mags had a flash of insight. "All we are talking about reminds me of a song by Steven Curtis Chapman."

"What's it called?" Zach asked.

"I think it's called *Do Everything*," Mags replied. Zach tapped the iTunes App on his phone. Within seconds, it had downloaded. The picture on his screen revealed it was from Chapman's project called *re•creation*. Zach pushed play and Steven Curtis' thumping guitar rhythms came to life.

> *You're picking up toys on the living room floor for the*
> *fifteenth time today*
> *Matching up socks, sweeping up lost cheerios that got away*
> *You put a baby on your hip, color on your lips and head out*
> *the door*
> *While I may not know you,*
> *I bet I know you*
> *Wonder sometimes, does it matter at all?*
>
> *Well let me remind you, it all matters just as long*
> *As you do everything you do to the glory of the One who*
> *made you,*
> *Cause he made you, to do every little thing that you do*
> *To bring a smile to his face*

Tell the story of grace
With every move that you make
And every little thing you do

Maybe you're that guy with the suit and tie, maybe your
shirt says your name
You may be hooking up mergers, cooking up burgers
But at the end of the day
Little stuff, big stuff
In between stuff
God sees it all the same
While I may not know you
I bet I know you
Wonder sometimes, does it matter at all?

Well let me remind you, it all matters just as long
As you do everything you do to the glory of the One who
made you,
Cause he made you, to do
Every little thing that you do
To bring a smile to his face
Tell the story of grace
With every move that you make
And every thing you do

Mags spoke in Zach's direction. "I think the poetic lines in this song should replace the *only one life* lines that have haunted you for so long. These lines are gloriously redemptive." Zach nodded in agreement.

Maybe you're sitting in math class
Or maybe on a mission in the Congo
Or maybe you're working at the office
Singing along with the radio
Maybe you're dining at a five-star
Or feeding orphans in the Myanmar
Anywhere and everywhere that you are

Whatever you do, it all matters
So do what you do
Don't ever forget
To do everything you do to the glory of the One who made
you,
Cause he made you
To do, every little thing that you do
To bring a smile to his face
And tell the story of grace

The three of them sat still, just reflecting as Chapman strummed out the final lines of the song. *What a remarkable synthesis of all I've been learning and all I want to be,* Zach thought.

Mags spoke in Zach's direction. "I think the poetic lines in this song should replace the *only one life* lines that have haunted you for so long. These lines are gloriously redemptive."

Zach nodded in agreement. "Say, that reminds me, I had a follow-up thought from the other night, from our big talk on Carver, Ford, and their work on alternate fuels."

"OK, what is it?" Gram asked.

"Oh, yes! Do tell, please," Mags replied, "we're waiting!" She said it with some ornery, mocking flirtation in her voice.

"Remember, Gram," Zach asked, "how you said I had brought our thoughts full circle, from the mystery letter, to the Congo where Grandpa Edgar and Grandma Lillian served, to Carver, and back to Henry Ford and Carver being friends?"

"Yes, I said that," Gram answered. "Full circle. That's where you brought the conversation, Grandson. Very well done! I love it when that happens in dialogue."

"*Almost,* Gram. *Almost* full circle." There was a rev of enthusiasm in Zach's voice, as if he had just discovered how to fuel his F-100 with water. He continued, "This thought hit me. If Ford and Carver spent that much time working together on such a creative project, there's little doubt in my mind. Henry Ford was encountering the glory of God as he interacted with George! Jesus' words from Matthew 5, remember Mags, and you know them, Gram. As kids back in Sunday School, we always quoted them right after singing *This Little Light of Mine*. We learned it in one of the older translations:

'Let your light so shine before men, that they may see your good works, and glorify your Father which is in heaven.' Since Carver was that passionate, to work for Christ's mission by serving others, he *had* to reveal God's glory to Henry Ford. I'm certain of it!"

Now Gram was smiling bigger than she had in three weeks. "And *that* idea is worth some more research, Grandson." She tossed him the Carver biography.

Just then, there was a humongous clap of thunder. They looked outside to discover howling wind, lightning, and the tops of trees were twisting. The three of them quickly took cover in the basement.

From their bunker, they could watch out the lower level sliding door. The storm was frighteningly severe. They anticipated that when they emerged from below, the yard would be full of tree limbs. When it finally subsided fifteen minutes later, they exited into the back yard through that basement sliding door. Sure enough, the yard was a mess. Gram began pacing 'round the back yard, and she started playing pick up sticks.

Mags and Zach wandered around front, and to their shock, they found one of the front yard trees had fallen directly across the hood of Zach's G37. The windshield, hood, and front fenders were all smashed.

The same tree had just missed falling on Henry's bed and tailgate. Just missed it.

"My dumb luck!" Zach declared as he surveyed the damage. He began feverishly running his fingers through his hair—a bundle of nervous energy. "Of course, it misses the old, ugly truck, and squashes my ten-month-old sports car."

"It's amazing luck, indeed!" Maggie exclaimed with great glee. And with a playful spin away from the demolished car, she stepped toward Zach. In all-out confidence, she stuck her fingers into his thick curly hair. She stepped even closer, pulled his head close, and she kissed him. It was far from a brother-sister kiss.

He grabbed her hands, and with no intention of stepping away, he held her close and kissed her again. Then he just stared into her great big eyes. It took him a few moments to find his words.

"Wow." Zach finally spoke. "Thanks for helping a guy take his mind off his totally demolished car. 'Certainly kind of you.'"

She laughed and smiled even bigger.

"So, please explain," Zach asked softly, still holding her close, "Exactly what do you think is so amazingly lucky about my car being crushed?"

"That's easy," Mags explained. "Now we get to drive Henry back to Pennsylvania. We'll just have to take him down to Marshall's right now. I'm sure he won't mind working on him between now and Monday. He's even more gloriously in love with the old fella than I am."

Zach shook his head and chuckled. Hand in hand, they walked toward Henry. And he seemed to be grinning from headlight to headlight.

The End

Reflecting on Henry's Story, God's Story, and Your Story

1. During the story, both Mags and Zach share their personal goals as they get ready to go back to Pennsylvania. List your top three personal goals as you wrap up your interaction with this story. Be specific and action-oriented related to both perspectives and behaviors you want to adopt at work.

2. What impresses you from Livingstone's speech at Cambridge? Name some implications for integration of faith and business.

3. What encourages your heart and mind from the *new glorious lines* of Chapman's song?

4. Review Zach's intentionality toward involvement with the new construction company in Haiti. What might intentionality look like for you related to exploration and potential involvement in some global business-mission endeavor? Describe what it might look like *for you* to engage in a global business endeavor.

5. Try your hand at writing a brief, two or three-chapter rendition of your own yet-to-come story. Envision and describe what your work, with God's grace and missional focus, might look like in the next five to ten years. Have fun writing the story, for his glory!

Next-Step Resources

God in the Marketplace: 45 Questions Fortune 500 Executives Ask About Faith, Life & Business, by Henry and Richard Blackaby (B&H, 2008)

The Heavenly Good of Earthly Work, by Darrell Cosden (Baker, 2006)

Culture Making: Recovering Our Creative Calling, by Andy Crouch (IVP, 2008)

The Integrated Life: Experience the Powerful Advantage of Integrating Your Faith and Work, by Ken Eldred (Manna Ventures, 2010)

Made to Matter: Devotions for Working Christians, by Randy Kilgore (Discovery House, 2008)

God's Pleasure at Work: Bridging the Sacred-Secular Divide, by Christian Overman (Ablaze, 2009)

The Other Six Days: Vocation, Work, and Ministry in Biblical Perspective, by R. Paul Stevens (Eerdmans, 1999)

Why Business Matters to God (and What Still Needs to Be Fixed), by Jeff Van Duzer (IVP 2010)

Work in the Spirit: Toward a Theology of Work, by Miroslav Volf (Wipf and Stock, 2001)

Work: A Kingdom Perspective on Labor, by Ben Witherington III (Eerdmans, 2011)

The Mission of God: Unlocking the Bible's Grand Narrative, by Christopher J. H. Wright (IVP, 2006)

Acknowledgements

I am deeply grateful to a wonderful team of people who generously supplied their loving cultivation and constant encouragement in order to help this project come to fruition.

Immense thanks to my wonderful wife, true love of my life, Nancy. She has cheered me on with great joy throughout the story's journey, granting me the graces of time, patience, and emotional support. She is such an amazing friend and gift from God on this adventure of missional living.

Christian and the entire team at Wipf and Stock—your enthusiasm for this project and your commitment to excellence made this resource much more compelling.

The leadership teams of Manor Church and Daybreak Community Church both supplied a remarkable investment of resources, anticipation, and joy in discovery.

My three amazing sons, Jarod, Joel, and Josiah, listened as I read the story a chapter at a time after dinner and then over breakfast at the shore. Your initial responsiveness and creative suggestions were so affirming.

Fifteen courageous adventurers participated in the original "book club" in order to experiment with reading, reflecting, and discussing the story. Great big thanks to Bruce, Tracy, John, Sarah, Todd, Ryan, Tracy, Matt, Michelle, Doug, Barb, Geoff, Jen, Brennen, and Ami. Your feedback and encouragement proved invaluable.

Years ago, Priscilla Zeller graciously taught a sixteen-year-old boy with clumsy fingers to type (on a vintage typewriter)—an ability I too often take for granted. Thanks for adding such skill to my life story. Virginia Mellring inspired me, teaching me to write with greater texture and depth of feeling. Zach, Mags, and Marshall are richer, more colorful characters because of you.

Dr. Friedhelm Loescher, Dr. James Lytle, Dr. John Lawlor, Dr. Gary Hauck, and Dr. Rembert Carter—you mentored me in thinking bigger, thinking biblically, and recognizing common grace in our Creator's loving plans for history.

Beth Graves and Kelli Risser granted marvelous proofreading and artistic design.

Great friends, Craig, Nate, David, and Bryan—your encouraging words across the entire adventure have been invaluable.

Dr. Paul Borden, Dr. Don Payne, Dr. David Osborn, and Dr. Terry Heisey—each of you supplied me with the motivation and resources to rise to higher places across this project. I am immensely grateful for such exceptional guidance.

Most importantly, my Savior, Friend, and Master, Jesus Christ, is worthy of my deepest gratitude and greatest glory.

About John Elton Pletcher

John is crazy about connecting with people over delicious coffee. He also enjoys running, watching movies, reading, playing baseball with his boys, and taking long walks with his golden retriever, Brodimus Maximus. John serves as lead pastor at Manor Church in Lancaster, Pennsylvania, and also teaches as adjunct faculty at Eastern University and Evangelical Seminary. He is married to Nancy, and they have three sons, Jarod, Joel and Josiah.

Pletch, as friends call him, holds the Doctor of Ministry in Leadership from Denver Seminary and the Master of Divinity from Baptist Bible Seminary (PA).

Passionate about helping leaders develop bigger hearts and skills for missional living, he is available for consultation, coaching, storytelling, and conference/seminar speaking during a limited number of days each year.

For further information about scheduling John for your event, plus reading his engaging blog and other creative resources, visit johneltonpletcher.com.

Thank you for helping advance God's great work! A portion of the profits from each copy of this book has been designated for helping start integrated, missional businesses in strategic new locations 'round the globe—all for God's glory.